IMPROVE YOUR
GOLF
THE PROFESSIONAL WAY

IMPROVE YOUR GOLF
THE PROFESSIONAL WAY

Ken Adwick

Ian Connelly

Alan Fine

John Jacobs

Beverly Lewis

Doubleday & Company, Inc.

Library of Congress Cataloging-in-Publication Data

Improve your golf the professional way

Includes index.
1. Golf. I. Jacobs, John, 1925-
GV965.P77 1987   796.352'3   87-440
ISBN 0-385-24210-7

Printed and bound in Italy by New Interlitho S.P.A. Milan

Contents

Chapter 1   **THE SET-UP**

The key to a good swing – *Connelly*	10-11
Learn to relax at address – *Lewis*	12-13
Adopt a good grip – *Lewis*	14-15
Calculating ball position – *Lewis*	16-17
Aiming in the right direction – *Lewis*	18-19
Loosen-up your golf muscles – *Jacobs*	20-21

Chapter 2   **THE SWING**

Why you need good tempo – *Connelly*	22-25
Swing the clubhead not yourself – *Connelly*	26-27
Swing sequences:	
Bernhard Langer	26-27
Nick Faldo & Bob Charles	28-29
Lee Trevino	30-31
Jack Nicklaus & Tom Watson	32-33
Severiano Ballesteros & Sandy Lyle	34-35
The inside attack – *Lewis*	36-37
The essence of a good swing – *Lewis*	38-41
Foot and leg action – *Lewis*	42-45

Chapter 3   **STRIKING**

The simple approach to impact – *Connelly*	46-47
Keep the violence out of your swing! – *Connelly*	48-49
Improve your driving – *Lewis*	50-53
Know your distance – *Lewis*	54-55
Know the laws of ball flight – *Jacobs*	56-57
Know your fairway woods – *Lewis*	58-61

Chapter 4   **THE SHORT GAME**

The secret of perfect chipping – *Lewis*	62-65
The up and over chip – *Lewis*	66-69
Mastering the long pitch – *Lewis*	70-73
Playing out of bunkers – *Lewis*	74-77
Judging bunker length – *Lewis*	78-81
Downhill bunker shots – *Lewis*	82-85
How to hole more putts – *Jacobs*	86-89
Two keys to better putting – *Jacobs*	90-91
Three tips to better putting – *Lewis*	92-93

Contents

Chapter 5   **CURING YOUR FAULTS**

The slice – *Jacobs*   94-95
The hook – *Jacobs*   96-97
How to avoid skying – *Adwick*   98-99
How to cure the push – *Adwick*   100-101
Toeing – the causes and
    the remedies – *Adwick*   102-105
How to avoid topping – *Jacobs*   106-107
How to stop hitting behind the ball – *Jacobs*   108-109
Cure your smother and get
    that ball up – *Adwick*   110-113
The myth of the late hit – *Adwick*   114-115
Groove your swing to eradicate
    the pull – *Adwick*   116-119
Avoiding an overswing – *Lewis*   120-123
Curing the shank – *Jacobs*   124-125

Chapter 6   **IMPROVING YOUR GAME**

When and how to shape your shots – *Jacobs*   126-127
How to combat uneven lies – *Adwick*   128-131
How to play from poor lies – *Adwick*   132-135
Getting out of trouble – *Adwick*   136-139
The correct way to hook and slice – *Adwick*   140-141
How to combat the advancing years – *Jacobs*   142-143
The point of practice – *Jacobs*   144-145
Practise your short game – *Jacobs*   146-147

Chapter 7   **THE MIND GAME**

Setting goals that are right for you – *Fine*   148-149
Conquer those first-tee nerves – *Fine*   150-151
Control your emotions and
    your scores – *Fine*   152-153
'Feel' your way to better shots – *Fine*   154-155
How your game can gain
    from competition – *Fine*   156-157

INDEX   158-159

ACKNOWLEDGEMENTS   160

Gary Player of South Africa, one of the all-time greats of golf

Chapter 1 THE SET-UP

Good golf starts from a sound foundation. How you set-up to the ball will determine ultimately the direction of your swing, so it is vital to get the foundations of the set-up correct. Yet, many golfers neglect this important aspect and continue to hit unsatisfactory shots as a result. Many of golf's familiar poor shots can be traced back to an incorrect set-up, so it is always worthwhile going back to the basics of the set-up to discover the cause of the fault. This chapter examines the fundamentals of grip, stance, ball position, aim and posture plus information on how to tone up your muscles for golf. Achieving the correct set-up position will require no great physical or athletic ability since it takes place before the club is actually set in motion. Once you have mastered the set-up, then you are well on the way to fulfilling your potential as a golfer.

The key to a good swing

You can only swing the club as well as you set-up to the ball, and if you set-up correctly you are far more likely to play consistently good golf. If you set-up *incorrectly* there is very little possibility of producing the shot you require.

If you watch the top professionals, either during a round or on the practice ground, you will notice the care and attention that they give to their pre-swing preparation. Look at the trouble Jack Nicklaus takes before each shot. He knows how important the set-up is; and all tournament players recognize that if something is wrong with their game then the fault most likely stems from the set-up and not from the actual swing.

In order to reach your full potential at golf, the foundations of grip and set-up must be correct, and developing these foundations requires no degree of skill or athleticism – it is merely a case of care and attention. Let us look therefore at the main factors governing the set-up position.

Posture

The easy way to adopt a correct posture is to stand with your back straight and your weight evenly distributed between your feet. Keeping your back straight, bend over from the waist just sufficiently to give your arms clearance from your body to allow for freedom of swing. Feel that your arms are simply hanging from your shoulders as opposed to being rigid. Flex your knees slightly and place your palms together. Then slide your right hand below the left as it would be positioned on the club.

If you follow the procedure above you will find, as a result of your right side being lower than the left that there is slightly more weight on the right side. You should also feel your weight more towards the balls of your feet.

For long and medium clubs, stand with your feet about shoulder-width apart (measured from the inside of your heels) and gradually narrow your stance for the shorter irons. Avoid extremes: too wide a stance will restrict your shoulder turn and leg action, while too narrow a stance will cause instability. Experiment to find what suits you and if you do happen to err, always make sure that it is on the narrow side.

It is impossible to stand too near the ball provided that your arms have sufficient clearance from your body to allow them to swing both back and through freely. Beware of crouching over the ball and setting your weight on the left side. This position will only encourage 'tilting' instead of turning the shoulders.

Always feel light or 'springy' as you set-up or, as Sam Snead calls it, 'oily'. Light and relaxed muscles will always propel the ball further than will heavy or tense muscles.

Aiming correctly

However good your swing, if you do not aim it correctly it loses most, if not all, of its effectiveness. Logic dictates that if your aim is bad, the only way you can hit the ball at the intended target is by introducing a compensatory error into your swing.

One of the best ways of learning to aim correctly is this: when you are on the practice ground lay two clubs on the ground, one parallel to your stance and the other at right angles to it. The club running parallel to feet and body will help you establish a square set-up, while the club running at right angles will help you to pinpoint the ball position.

It is vital to remember that your

1 An ideal set-up. The head and the upper body are positioned behind the ball

2 The right side is lower and more passive than the left as is shown by the slightly flexed right arm

3 The right knee is cocked towards the target to give the backswing support and stability

4 The ball position is two inches inside the left heel and the left arm and shaft are in line

body line runs to the left of the target, so that if you look directly over your left shoulder you are actually looking to the left of your target. If you look over your left shoulder and see the target directly on that line, then you are probably aiming to the right. This will mean also that your clubhead is aiming in that direction. In the ensuing pages of this section on the set-up, we shall examine in more detail the factors connected with the address position, for it is only by adopting the correct habits at the outset that your game can succeed. If you look like a good player when you stand to the ball, then you have an excellent chance of playing like one.

Learn to relax at address

Unlike most other sports, golf is played from a stationary position, the positive side being that it gives you time to adopt the correct set-up, within a fairly generous time limit. However, the negative side to this situation is that the longer you stand at the ball the more tense you may become, and this tension leads to the muscles tightening. Any changes you choose to make in your address position may feel uncomfortable, and this, in turn, can create tension.

The muscles that suffer most from this tension are those in the upper body, especially in the shoulders, arms and hands. The shoulders become hunched, and make it very difficult to turn sufficiently in the backswing. The arms tend to be too straight at address, making it impossible for them to create the necessary swinging motion in the backswing. And if the hands grip the club too tightly, the forearms will tense, and the power that the hands should release on the downswing will be lost. All these examples lead to a stifled, short and jerky swing, instead of one that is full and flows smoothly.

Pre-shot routines

One of the ways to remain in a relaxed yet prepared state at address is to have a fairly strict pre-shot routine, which should be used also when practising. Having visualized the shot you wish to play, select your club and, with a light grip, take a practice swing. This serves three purposes. Firstly, it will accustom you to how the club feels, which is important. For instance, a driver and wedge have a very different feel about them when

Seve Ballesteros demonstrating a relaxed address: the shoulders are dropped, arms hanging loosely, the upper arms close to the body. This position enables the arms to swing easily without power being generated by the shoulders

swung. Secondly, it will give you the chance to swing the club in a manner that will produce the shot that you have visualized, maybe a fade or a punched shot, and, thirdly, it does help to prepare the muscles for the job in hand, and encourage them to stay relaxed.

Posture

When you set-up to the ball, always make sure that you bend over sufficiently from the hips, creating space for your arms to hang down in front of you in a relaxed manner. Many players keep their backs too erect at address, and then the only way to get the club to the ground is to arch their wrists, which sets up a chain reaction of straightening their arms and hunching their shoulders. As explained earlier, this is no way to prepare.

Pre-shot movements

Whilst setting up to the ball, you should be keeping in mind a picture of where you want the ball to fly, and this should be backed up by one or two glances towards that target. However, the important thing to bear in mind is that if one or two glances are sufficient for the easy shots, then you have to keep to that number for the more difficult ones, too. Should you start taking four or five looks down the fairway, you will be telling your body that this is a different situation from normal, and there is every chance that you will create tension. Most professionals build into their pre-shot routine a waggle of the clubhead, using just the hands and forearms. This movement is designed to prevent them becoming too static at address, and also serves as a rehearsal for how the clubhead will move in the first few feet of the swing. Ideally you should also have a trigger movement that gets your swing started, maybe a forward press with your hands, or a slight kick-in of the right knee like Gary Player. The type of move itself is not important but it serves as a signal to the rest of your body to commence the swing.

Ben Crenshaw at address with a wedge. Note how the ball has been positioned towards the back of the stance

Tall players can make the mistake of crouching over the ball at address which causes tension. Nick Faldo shows how a tall player should stand to the ball — no evidence of hunching the shoulders here

Adopt a good grip

I t would be fair to say that there are very few really good golfers who have a so-called bad grip. Certainly the best professionals in the world have a variety of grip positions, according to how they wish to hit the ball. However, these positions all fall within certain guidelines.

For the beginner, trying to adopt a good grip is perhaps one of the most difficult parts of golf, but if learned in the early stages, it will be a solid foundation on which to build his game. Any changes made by a teacher tend to feel uncomfortable, and the only way to overcome the unfamiliar feel of the new grip is to practise not only hitting shots but also just gripping and regripping the club without hitting the ball, and eventually the new, correct grip will feel natural.

The purpose of the grip is to return the clubhead back to the ball in a square position, without having to manipulate or use your hands excessively. If your grip does not allow you to square the clubhead at impact, it is quite probable that you will start to build compensating factors into your swing. So get the grip right, and you stand a good chance of developing a sound swing.

Left hand

For the right-handed player, this is the guiding, or leading, hand in the swing, and thus it is placed on the grip in such a way that some firmness is created. With the clubface square to

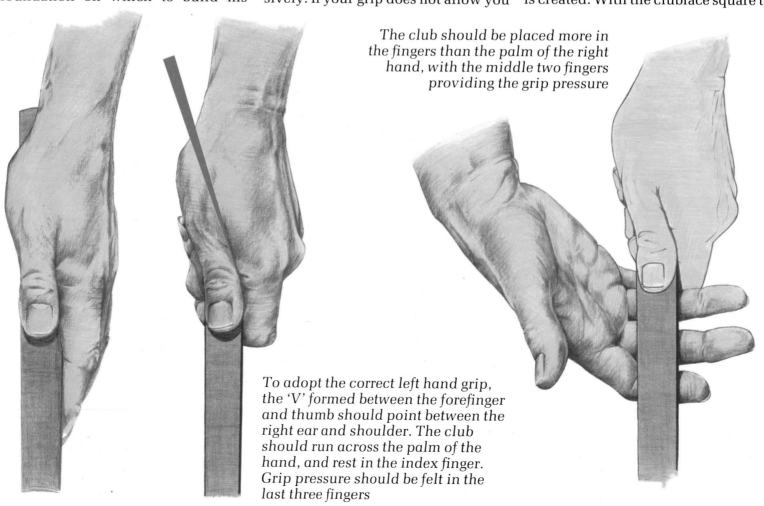

The club should be placed more in the fingers than the palm of the right hand, with the middle two fingers providing the grip pressure

To adopt the correct left hand grip, the 'V' formed between the forefinger and thumb should point between the right ear and shoulder. The club should run across the palm of the hand, and rest in the index finger. Grip pressure should be felt in the last three fingers

your intended target, the end of the grip is placed underneath the fleshy pad at the heel of the hand, and then across the palm and the first finger. It lies in a diagonal position across the hand, rather than straight across the base of the fingers, which would not give a sufficiently firm support. As the hand closes on the grip, the thumb rests just to the right-hand side of the

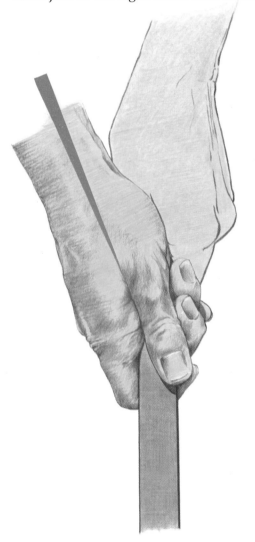

centre of the grip, and is neither stretched down the shaft nor pulled up in any way. The 'V' formed between the thumb and forefinger should point between your chin and right shoulder. You should also be able to see at least two knuckles of your hand when you look down. The last three fingers are the ones that grip the club, thus bringing the muscles in the back of the arm into play.

Right hand
As the left hand is the guide, so the right hand provides the power, and is therefore placed on the grip in a slightly different way to allow this to happen. Whereas with the left hand the grip was placed in the palm and fingers, with the right hand the club sits more towards the base of the fingers, which allows the hand to be more active at impact. In fact, the right hand grips the club in much the same manner as you would grip a stone that you were about to throw. The hollow of the palm of the hand

In the completed grip the 'V' on the right hand points parallel to the left, to a point between the right ear and shoulder. When viewed from the front, none of the left thumb should be visible, and the right thumb lies just left of centre on the shaft

fits snugly over the left thumb, and if you were to view the grip in a mirror, you should not be able to see the left thumb at all. The right forefinger should be triggered on the shaft, which helps to prevent the hand getting too far under the grip, and the thumb should rest just to the left-hand side of the centre of the grip. The 'V' created between the forefinger and thumb should point parallel to that of the left hand, and the middle two fingers should apply all the pressure.

Whether you overlap the little finger of the right hand onto the forefinger of the left – the Vardon grip interlocks these two fingers, as does Jack Nicklaus – or have both hands completely on the grip, is a matter of preference, but in each case, the hands should be placed in such a way as to make them work together as much as possible.

Grip pressure
Grip pressure is one of the most important points to consider, and one of the most difficult to define, but generally speaking, more people grip the club too tightly, than too loosely. The grip should feel light at address, and will naturally tighten slightly under the weight of the club during the backswing.

Clubface reaction
If both hands are placed in such a way that the two 'V's point too much towards the chin, the clubface will be returned to the ball in an open position, i.e. looking right of your target, and the ball will curve in that direction. Alternatively, hands placed too much under the grip, resulting in the 'V's pointing outside the right shoulder, will close the clubface at impact, and the ball will curve to the left.

The correct grip position for each person will vary according to how much hand action is employed naturally, i.e. little with the beginner, but increasing with the better player. So if your shots curve viciously to either right or left, first check your grip.

Calculating ball position

When determining the correct ball position, you have to consider the angle of attack you need to produce the desired result. To get an iron shot airborne, you must hit in a downwards direction, whereas a fairway wood needs to be swept from the grass a little more. A driver also needs to be swept away or even hit when the clubhead is starting to move on an upward path. So in order to hit the ball with the right angle of attack, you must position the ball in a different spot in relation to your feet, depending on the club you are hitting.

Short irons
First, and let us assume that in the following examples you have a standard lie, we will deal with a short iron, say an 8-, which will be swung in a fairly upright manner. Take your address position, with your feet together, and the back of the ball opposite the centre of your feet. Now move your left

foot about 3 to 4 inches to the left, and your right foot about 5 or 6 inches to the right. From this fairly narrow stance, you are in a good position to hit the ball while the clubhead is still on its descending path. Because an 8-iron is a short club, it will be swung on a more upright plane than a middle iron, and you can therefore expect to take a fair-sized divot.

Middle irons
The same procedure should be adopted with middle irons, say a 5-. With your feet together, move your left foot about 3 to 4 inches to the left, but this time move your right foot slightly further to the right, maybe 8 or 9 inches. The ball now will look further forward in your stance than it did with the 8-iron, which really is the case. However, it is still in the same position as before in relation to your left foot. You will still hit the ball during the downward part of the

clubhead's journey, but because you are using a longer shafted club, do not expect to take a large divot.

Long irons
Using long irons, follow the same pattern, moving your right foot just a little further to the right. But since long irons are swung on a flatter plane than either middle or short irons, this time you will be less likely to take a divot – just the top layer of grass may be removed instead.

It is recommended that you hit all iron shots with the ball in the same position in relation to your left foot. It is the right foot that moves in graduated distances to the right according to which club you are hitting. If, using the above distances as your guideline, you are still not getting a well struck iron shot with a ball then turf contact, experiment by moving the ball back a little more in your stance. Certainly the real beginner should play the ball

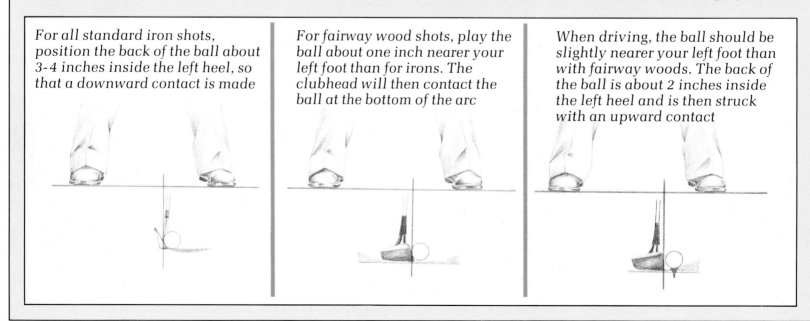

For all standard iron shots, position the back of the ball about 3-4 inches inside the left heel, so that a downward contact is made

For fairway wood shots, play the ball about one inch nearer your left foot than for irons. The clubhead will then contact the ball at the bottom of the arc

When driving, the ball should be slightly nearer your left foot than with fairway woods. The back of the ball is about 2 inches inside the left heel and is then struck with an upward contact

nearer the centre of his/her feet, until such time that upper body movement becomes co-ordinated with the correct leg action.

Fairway woods

When playing fairway woods, you want to contact the ball at the bottom of the swing arc, thus allowing you to sweep the ball from the turf. Since you have now found out the correct position for the ball when hitting iron shots, you can work from there. With your feet together, and the ball opposite the middle of your feet, move your left foot approximately 1 inch less to the left than before, and your right foot about the same distance as for a long iron. The ball has now moved forward in your stance, and should coincide with the bottom of the arc. Again, a little time spent experimenting on exactly where the ball should be is well worthwhile.

The driver

Now that you have found the bottom of the swing arc, it should be easy to position the ball correctly for the driver, or whichever club you use for driving. From the set-up, you should place your left foot just slightly less to the left than with the fairway woods. You will find that the back of the ball is approximately 2 inches inside your left heel. You are now assured of hitting the ball at the bottom of the swing arc, or ideally just slightly on the up-swing. Because the driver is the longest club in the bag, the attack on the ball will be shallow, since you swing on a flatter plane. However, many players swing too steeply with this club, resulting in a skied, smothered or weak, fading shot.

Bad lies

When you are confronted with a shot from a bad lie, you will need a steeper angle of attack on the ball, and the way to achieve this is to put the ball back at address, nearer your right foot. Positioned here, the clubhead is on a steep downward path when contact is made, but there are two points

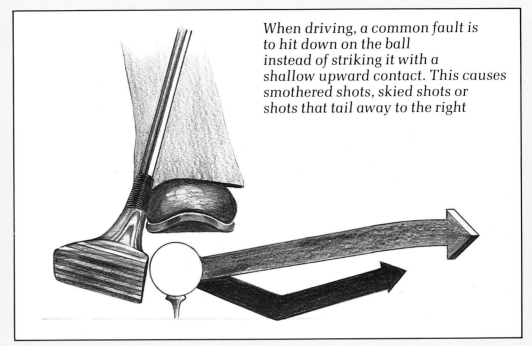

When driving, a common fault is to hit down on the ball instead of striking it with a shallow upward contact. This causes smothered shots, skied shots or shots that tail away to the right

to consider when making this adjustment. Firstly, since the club is still on its way down, it is also travelling towards the ball from inside the ball to target line and therefore there is every chance that the ball may fly to the right, so you should allow for this. Secondly, when you position the ball back, it also means that you are taking effective loft off the club, so a 7-iron may become more like an 8-iron, depending on how far back you put the ball. It is also worth remembering that if shots from standard lies are well struck but flying right, the ball may be too near the centre of your stance.

Very good lies

Should you be lucky enough to find the ball really sitting up either on the fairway or in the rough, you will then want to sweep the ball away, so position it slightly nearer your left foot than normal. This will move it towards the bottom of the arc and help to produce the shallow attack on the ball that is needed. However, now that it is forward, it will be contacted when the clubhead is starting to move back inside the ball to target line, and so the shot may go slightly left. You

will also have more effective loft on the club, so a 4-iron may react like a 5-iron. Again, if your shots from standard lies always start left, you may have the ball too far forward.

With the ball too far forward, contact is made when the clubhead is swinging to the left of the target. With the ball too far back, contact is made when the clubhead is moving to the right of the target

Aiming in the right direction

Aiming yourself in the right direction may sound an easy task – so easy, in fact, that many players become careless about it – but at an instruction school in the United States, the teachers found that 90 per cent of their pupils aimed, or set-up incorrectly, with 80 per cent of them aiming their clubface, or body to the right. Consequently what tends to happen is that you start to build compensation into the swing, in order to get the ball back on target.

The best way to line up correctly is first to understand that the body and the clubface are not aimed at the same point. Whilst the clubface points towards the target, your body should aim parallel but left of this spot. This is best illustrated perhaps by imagining a railway track – while the clubhead and ball are on one rail, you are standing on the other.

The correct routine

To achieve correct alignment, first stand behind the ball, looking towards the target. Now pick out a spot, perhaps a divot, or a daisy, about 15 to 30 inches ahead of the ball on the target line. Walk round to the side of the ball, and place the clubhead down so that it aims from the ball over your intermediate target. You should draw a mental picture of a line from this mark back to the ball and then set

To help you line up correctly, imagine that you are standing on the nearside rail of a set of railway lines, while the ball is on the far rail. Your feet, knees, hips, shoulders and eyes should be parallel to the track, and thus the ball to target line

Bernard Hunt shows how practising with clubs laid on the ground can help with alignment

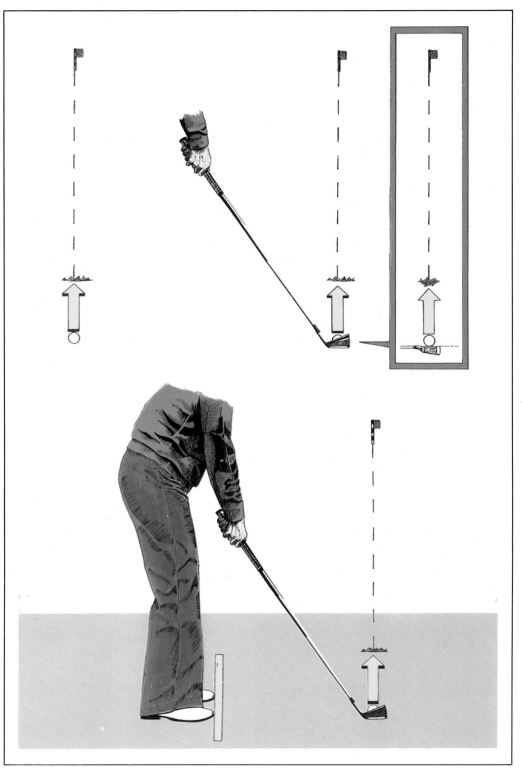

your body parallel to this. First get your shoulders positioned correctly, then work downwards to the forearms, hips, knees and, finally, your feet. It is also important to have your eyes on this same parallel line, or visual distortion will make lining up more difficult.

If aiming correctly is a problem, you will find that using an intermediate target will benefit your short game and putting as well, although with these shots you may wish to have your hips and feet slightly open.

Practice tips

One of the best ways to practise your lining-up is to put your clubs on the ground. When out on the course, use an intermediate target since it is easier to aim over a yard, rather than 150 yards. You may also find it helpful to have someone check your aim by placing a club across your shoulders once you have taken your address position. Remember, though, that this club should point parallel to the target and not at it.

To help your alignment, stand behind the ball, and pick out an intermediate target about 2 to 3 feet ahead of the ball, on the target line. As you address the ball, use this target to help you set yourself parallel to the ball to target line

Loosen-up your golf muscles

In order of priority, the main requirements for playing really good golf are as follows:

1 Temperament,
2 A repeating sound method,
3 Physical fitness and strength.

All of these requirements need to be worked on to achieve consistency and high standards. The efforts we make to achieve a better temperament and method are not always rewarded as we would wish, whereas to be better equipped physically is usually just hard work. The best exercise of all is practice during which time the golf muscles are being used. However, it is particularly in the winter months that efforts can and should be made to get and keep as fit as possible, especially if bad weather stops you playing golf.

To be fit and enjoy the feeling of well-being that comes naturally with fitness is obviously desirable for all activities, but, regarding golf, the hands, wrists, forearms and the legs should receive special attention. If you spend a great deal of time travelling in your car or have a sedentary office job, then keep a squash ball handy and squeeze it whenever you get the chance (not when you are driving, though!). This will help to strengthen your hands and wrists.

The best exercise for strengthening your forearms is to wind up a weight attached to a smooth, circular piece of wood. Tie a strong 90cm/36in length of cord to the weight and then pin it to the piece of wood. Stand with your arms extended straight out in front of you and slowly wind up the weight. This exercise not only strengthens your forearms but aids the wrist and hand action when you come to swing a club.

To strengthen your legs, sit in a chair with your legs stretched out in front of you with weights resting on your ankles. Now, slowly lift and lower your legs. To condition your leg muscles rather than build them up, it is better to lift a heavy weight a few times rather than to lift a light weight a number of times.

The simple exercise of skipping is also obviously beneficial with the added advantage that the lungs and respiratory system also receive attention. Jogging can be aerobically beneficial, too, but is more enjoyable if you have a companion to run with you. Start off slowly and do not attempt too much too soon. Competitive games of squash or badminton are an enjoyable way of maintaining fitness as the competitive element makes it easier to push yourself to the limits of endurance. However, they must be played regularly if you are to receive lasting fitness benefits.

Squeezing a small, soft ball, like a squash ball, at every available opportunity is a good way to strengthen the hands and wrists

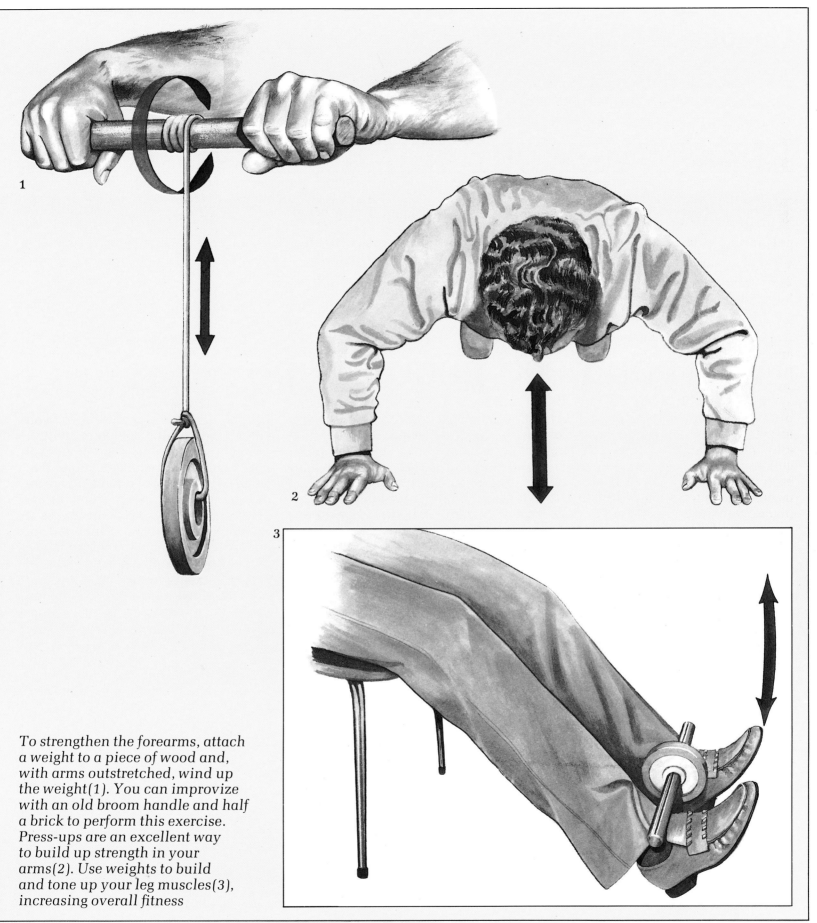

To strengthen the forearms, attach a weight to a piece of wood and, with arms outstretched, wind up the weight(1). You can improvize with an old broom handle and half a brick to perform this exercise. Press-ups are an excellent way to build up strength in your arms(2). Use weights to build and tone up your leg muscles(3), increasing overall fitness

Chapter 2 THE SWING

As the word implies, the swing is a continuous action which allows the golfer to create momentum and speed which can be delivered, via the clubhead, to the ball. The golf swing is not a hit, lunge or a bash – it is a very graceful movement which is designed to create the maximum clubhead speed in a balanced rhythmic manner. In creating this balance and rhythm, the movements of the swing have to be co-ordinated in the correct sequence. This chapter tells you how you can achieve this with the emphasis placed on the tempo of the swing so that these movements have time to take place. A good golf swing, one that consistently delivers the clubhead to the ball square to the line of flight, is founded on a correct set-up and a smooth, flowing action with the minimum of real effort. There is advice on how to hit the ball further, and feet and leg action.

Why you need good tempo

Control is the essence of good golf and your tempo largely determines the measure of control you achieve. The pace of swing at which you can generate clubhead speed under control is the tempo best suited to you. You should swing only as fast or with as much effort as your hands and arms can control the clubhead comfortably.

Effortless power
Most players tend to equate distance with effort, but this is false. Top-class players hit the ball a long way without any apparent effort. This is because all the energy is transmitted to the clubhead, and they know that bodily effort has an adverse effect on the swing.

How many times have you struck a drive miles down the middle and one of your playing companions has remarked, "You didn't seem to put any effort into that one"? The reason your companion made that remark was because it was true! Inevitably, when you step on the next tee, you think that you will apply a little more effort and produce an even better shot and, equally inevitably, you do not. If

anything, you should have swung with even less effort.

Another example would be when you have had to play a long shot to lay up short of a hazard – possibly a lake in front of the green. It is a situation where it does not matter if you are 10 yards short or 20 yards short – maximum distance is not a priority. It is such an easy shot with nothing at stake that all you do is take a smooth, easy swing at the ball only to find that the ball takes off like a rocket and plunges into the water. This is an example of distance being achieved without conscious effort because distance was not the prime thought occupying your mind.

Backswing
The purpose of the backswing is no more and no less than to put the player in a position to make the downswing. Most golfers take the club back (as opposed to swinging it back) too quickly, chiefly because they feel that the faster they go back, the more clubhead speed is generated on the way down. This is a fallacy. An over-fast backswing is usually the result of too much tension at address,

usually caused by anxiety. You should swing the club back with a feeling of lightness in the grip pressure and lightness in the arms. Remember, the pace of the backswing should only be such as will allow maximum control during the change of direction.

Stifle the hit impulse
When a swing breaks down, more often than not it is at the point when the swing direction is changing from going back to coming down. This is caused mainly by an over-fast backswing, but also by an uncontrollable urge to hit at the ball instead of swinging through it. The result is loss of control by the left side and a successful takeover led by the right side. This alters the path of the swing and the position of the clubface to the detriment of the shot. The remedy lies in the words of Bobby Jones: "A golf club should not only be swung back leisurely, it should also be swung down leisurely".

Through impact: the clubhead continues to gradually build up acceleration with the ball merely being in the way as opposed to being hit at.

1

2

3

4

5

6

One of the longest and straightest drivers in the world, Greg Norman creates maximum clubhead speed by maintaining a smooth tempo. An unhurried, one-piece takeaway shows the club shaft as a virtual extension of the left arm(1). As the hands and arms continue to carry the club upwards(2), the left shoulder is beginning to turn to allow Norman to reach a fully coiled position at the top of the swing(3). Just prior to impact(4) and Norman shows that there has been no attempt to hit 'at' the ball as the club is being delivered squarely into the back of the ball. After impact(5) and the clubhead is released freely through the shot and the impetus of the swing carries him on to a full finish(6)

Why you need good tempo

1

2

3

Completion of swing: if the pace of your swing is controlled, you will finish in control of your balance and you should be able to hold your finish indefinitely.

Good tempo does not mean slow
All great players have good tempo but that does not mean that they all swing at the same speed. They develop their own best tempo through an instinctive sense of control and timing.

Compare the tempo of Nick Faldo with that of Tom Watson, for instance. Faldo's most admired swing trait is his smooth, even, slowish tempo. Even when his swing is out of sorts, his tempo has saved him by giving him time to make 'in swing' corrections through a fine sense of touch and feel. On the other hand, Watson has a much quicker tempo, although it looks faster than it actually is. In relation to the rest of his

swing Watson makes a relatively slow backswing, has an easy-paced change of direction and gradually builds up the speed on the downswing. Some players, such as Sam Snead, Ben Crenshaw, Brian Barnes and Sam Torrance, have slow tempos whereas others like Lanny Wadkins and Brian Waites have quick tempos. However, what they all have in common is a tempo that suits them as individuals and is effective in their game.

Gary Player would be regarded as having a quick tempo but it is one that suits him and very few people would argue with his record over the past 25 years. His address position(1) is full of exaggerated good points and from here he achieves a perfect position at the top of the swing(2) with the club shaft pointing at the target. Starting down(3) and already the right leg is beginning to drive towards the ball. Approaching impact(4) and the right arm is hugging the body and then begins to extend as the ball is on its way(5 and 6). The follow-through is poised(7), proof that he has remained in control of the club throughout the stroke

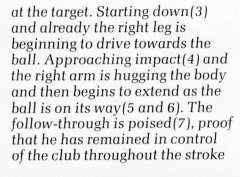

Tempo tips

1 Feel that your pace of swing is the same back and down.

2 Try to swing your driver at the same tempo as you swing your 9-iron.

3 Try hitting a 7-iron about 70 yards with a full swing. You will find that you will hit the ball twice as far because you are in control.

4 Overcoming the hit impulse is a major step towards establishing the pace of swing that is right for you. Swing through the ball, *not* at it.

5 Practise 'swishing' the clubhead. As a 'swish' is created by clubhead speed and it is this that you are looking for at impact, your instinct will discover the best tempo in order to achieve this.

6 Feel light at address and free from undue tension – this will help your tempo enormously.

Swing the clubhead... not yourself

1

2

3

The golf action is called a swing – not a hit, bash or lunge. The very term conjures up such words as 'smooth', 'rhythmic', 'fluent', 'continuous' and 'feel'. This sense of 'feel' should be transmitted to the clubhead as you cannot really swing something without feeling it.

The basic objective in golf is to swing the clubhead forwards in order to propel the ball forwards – good players do just that, whereas not-so-good players tend to swing themselves around and not the clubhead forwards. No matter which method you use, what the ball does is dependent entirely on what you do with the clubhead.

When you look at the great players, you never see a deliberate movement from position to position. Instead, you will notice a continuous, free-flowing movement back and through the ball. Certainly, positions are important but they must never take priority over free swinging of the hands and arms. The great players swing *through* positions; they do not actually try and achieve them during a swing – there simply is not time to do so.

The swing – a brief description

A brief overall description of the swing would be as follows: stand to the ball free from undue tension, especially in the upper body, gripping the club with lightness and sensitivity in mind. Now swing the clubhead back with the arms in a smooth, unhurried movement, allowing the left shoulder to be pulled to a turn.

Then, in a similar smooth, unhurried fashion, swing the clubhead down and forwards with the arms, allowing the right shoulder to be pulled under and through to the finish. Thus the arms do the swinging and the body responds to the arm swing.

The most fundamental action in golf is the swinging of the clubhead through feel in the hands and motion in the arms. A very good training exercise for this is to stand with your feet close together and hit shots simply by swinging your arms back and through. There is no need to worry about your hips or shoulders or anything else as they will respond automatically. Always bear in mind that swing your arms is a simple concept, and if your concept is simple then your swing will be, too.

The 1985 US Masters champion, Bernhard Langer uses his arms to create maximum leverage and power through the swing. Langer's power stems from an aggressive pulling action of his left arm and leg through the ball. At address(1), Langer starts the club back smoothly and then begins to extend the club away from the ball(2) to create the maximum arc.

At the top of the swing(3) he starts the pulling action down into the ball while his left arm still maintains the width of arc he has created(4). Approaching impact and his upper body still remains behind the ball(5) while his arms continue to swing forward and bring the clubhead into the ball at a position that all golfers should try and emulate(6)

4

5

6

Nick Faldo

Maintaining his wonderfully drowsy rhythm allows Nick Faldo to fully control the club throughout the swing and control of the club means control of the ball. In this picture

sequence, Faldo demonstrates a full swing with an iron which shows how the swinging of the club creates the correct movements in

Bob Charles

Simplicity is the key to Bob Charles' swing and although the tall New Zealander remains the only left-hander to have won the Open

Championship, his swing, if mirrored, would contain all of the good points of a right-handed Open Champion. From address, Charles simply takes

the lower body. For many club golfers it is the other way round. Swinging the club back pulls the left side towards the right leg and

swinging the club down pulls the right side towards the left to provide effort-less power rather than powerless effort

the club back smoothly to the top of the swing allowing the arms to dictate the lower body movements and then brings the club back down again.

There is no attempt to hit 'at' the ball, it is merely in the way of the clubhead and is dispatched with the minimum of effort

Lee Trevino

The master of ball flight and control, Lee Trevino's address position(1) reveals that although his feet and hips are open to the target line, his shoulders are square to that line. As he starts the club back(2) the left knee is being pulled inwards(3) as the hands continue upwards. At the top of the swing(4) the legs are poised to provide the powerful drive through the ball(5) and the hands have dropped the club back inside the target line. Just after impact(6) the ball is on its way and on to a typical Trevino finish(7). Trevino is immensely strong, particularly in the legs and this enables him to keep the clubface driving towards the target and create the familiar fading pattern to his shots

7

Jack Nicklaus

Jack Nicklaus on the practice ground at Augusta National, home of the US Masters, an event Nicklaus has won five times. At address for this short iron shot, Nicklaus lets his arms hang freely down and initiates the swing with that familiar turning of the head to the right. From the top of the swing he drops the club back into the ball, allowing the momentum he has built up to release the clubhead through and on to a balanced finish

Tom Watson

Tom Watson on the practice ground at Royal Birkdale, site of his fifth Open Championship victory in 1983. Watson is extremely strong in the forearms and a very aggressive striker through the ball, using his arms to generate clubhead speed. However, there is no loss of control or balance through this short iron shot as he makes a full turn and delivers the clubhead into the ball with telling effect

Severiano Ballesteros

Since Seve Ballesteros first burst onto the scene in the 1976 Open Championship at the age of 19, his swing has developed into a more controlled action. Points to look for in this sequence are the relaxed address position(1) and the smooth takeaway(2) which enables him to reach a fully coiled position at the top of the swing(3) without any extraneous movement. Approaching impact(4) and Ballesteros has maintained the angle between the left arm and the shaft and is poised to release the clubhead through the ball(5) to a relaxed finish(6)

Sandy Lyle

In this sequence Sandy Lyle, the 1985 Open Champion, demonstrates his mastery of the long irons. At address(1) he is relaxed with the arms extended. The start of the swing(2) shows how quickly he gets the club back inside to the target line as his shoulders, arms and club turn away from the ball in one unit. This puts him in a perfect position halfway back(3) with arms, shoulders and club shaft in a perfect plane. Coming down into the ball(4), note how the club-head has stayed inside the left arm line. After impact(5), the left side has cleared to make room for the club to swing down the line of the target and back inside the line again to a poised finish(6)

1

2

3

4

5

6

The inside attack

In order to hit the ball directly towards the target, the club must be swinging straight down the ball to target line at impact, and the clubface must be square to that line. However, if you are standing to the side of the ball, it is not possible to swing the clubhead straight back and down that ball to target line for very long, before it has to move inside. If you were standing with the ball about two or three inches from your feet, similar to putting, you could swing the club on a straight line throughout the swing, but it would lack power and there would be too steep an angle of attack on the ball. But by swinging the clubhead from the correct address position, up and inside and the backswing, you can return it on a similar downward path and can release the hand and arms during the strike, thus maximizing your power potential.

Incorrect right side power

Many golfers ruin what could be a good swing because they fail to return to the ball from the inside on the way down. Perhaps having made a reasonably good backswing, with an adequate shoulder turn, they feel most of the power is in the right side and shoulder, and immediately want to use that power. The clubhead is then thrown outside the correct downswing path and approaches the ball on a steep outside-in trajectory. The ball must then start left of the target and, in order to compensate for the first error, the golfer has to block the hands, leaving the clubface open, which will spin the ball back somewhere towards the target. The outcome is a weak glancing blow that lacks distance and accuracy. It is easy to understand how this problem arises. Most people who play golf right-handed are right-handed, and all their lives the left hand and arm have done little, and are therefore not as strong or developed as the right. When they swing the club, naturally the right side wants to dominate, and never more so than at the top of the backswing. From even a fairly good backswing position, to the average player the right shoulder area feels more powerful and it cannot wait to 'have a go' at the ball. As explained, this produces exactly the wrong attack on the ball and is an error in the swing that should be altered before it becomes too ingrained.

Left for control, right for power

Since it is the strongest side, it is the right hand and arm that provide most of the power, but it must be matched in its contribution to the swing by the guiding element of the left arm. As already established, this, for the naturally right-handed golfer (as opposed to the left-handed person playing right-handed), is the weak part of the swing. It would be advisable for any player wishing to reach his full potential to develop his left hand and arm so that they become as strong as the right. One of the best exercises is to swing the club just with the left arm, starting by gripping well down the shaft on a 5-iron, and just swinging halfway back and through on the correct inside to inside path for perhaps five minutes a day. Make certain that at the end of the backswing and throughswing, the toe (not the face) of the club points to the sky as this indicates that the clubhead is square to the swing path.

This routine not only strengthens the left arm, but educates it in its role in the swing, without interference from the right side. As you get stronger, the swing should be lengthened, and the club held nearer the end of the shaft. Attention should be paid to ensuring that the change of direction at the top of the swing is carried out smoothly and without any hurry, since to rush at this point might well throw the swing out of line. Having spent five or 10 minutes on one-armed practice, replace your right hand and make a swing. You will now start to feel how much more the left arm is controlling the club and giving the right side guidance. If you were to break down the role played by each hand and arm, it is the left that swings the clubhead away and is responsible for the change of direction at the top of the swing. From that point onwards, both right and left provide the power, with the left still controlling the direction.

How to let the swing work

Once you have achieved a certain degree of control with the left arm, it is still important to allow that control to be used fully in the swing without the right shoulder wanting to take over. If you can make a fairly sound backswing, where the shoulders are turned about 90 degrees, weight is mainly on the right leg, and the club is virtually parallel to the target line, you are in a good position to swing the club down on the inside. Your first movement should be to swing your arms down with the feeling that

your back is still turned to the target. You must also transfer your weight back to your left side, so that your hips can start to clear, making room for your arms to swing through.

To the golfer who has spent his time swinging from out-to-in, this movement will feel as though you are hitting the ball well to the right, and this may possibly happen. In an attempt to get the ball on target from the old out-to-in swing path, the hand action was blocked through impact, so that the clubface was open, thus slicing the ball back somewhere near the target. But to match the inside to straight to inside swing path that you have now achieved, you must allow the wrists, hands and arms to release the clubhead through impact.

This in itself may well need some closer attention, and one of the best exercises to promote a freer wrist action

is, using an iron, to take a very short backswing, where the hands only reach waist height and then hit the ball as hard as you can, allowing your hands to provide the strike and your arms to rotate through the impact area. The follow-through should only be as long as the backswing, and the whole action may feel rather loose and uncontrolled. But all feelings in golf are relative, and since up until this time the hand, arm and wrist actions have been stifled, this is only to be expected. However, this new-found freedom will enable the club-face to be returned squarely to the line of the swing, which will result in a straight shot. While you are practising this drill, it will help if you sit the ball on a low tee peg.

Let the clubhead be your guide
The golfer who is better able to feel

Nick Price's perfect posture provides ample space for his arms to hang naturally, and to move easily to the inside as his backswing progresses. From an ideal top of the backswing position, his legs initiate the change of direction, so that the clubhead remains on an inside path back to the ball. After impact, it can be seen that the right hand and arm are rotating over the left, as a result of the hands and arms releasing fully through the impact area

where the clubhead is swung may be able to convert himself from an 'out-to-in' to 'in-to-in' swinger, by visualizing the line along which the clubhead should be swung. This should first be practised without the ball, and perhaps with the aid of tee pegs indicating the correct path.

The essence of a good swing

When starting to play golf, you have to learn how different parts of your body should move and react in order to build a sound swing. Time often has to be spent learning an individual movement or position, which, once practised, gradually becomes more natural. When this happens, you can begin to work on another aspect of the swing, and thus gradually build one that can be reproduced without too much conscious thought. However, you must always remember that golf is not a series of positions, but a continuous swinging movement of the clubhead on a swing path that will send the ball in the desired direction.

One good thing leads to another

To achieve this ideal, a good grip is essential, and the better the set-up, the more likely you are to make an effective backswing. In turn, the better the backswing you make, the more likely you are to swing the clubhead down on the correct path and angle. The better your foot and leg action, the more likely you are to hit through the ball and not just at it. So it is quite obvious that the individual parts of the swing are inter-related, and thus in developing your game, you should try to improve all departments equally as you progress.

How the swing works

In a good golf swing, the hands and arms swing the club, and the body plays its part by responding to this

Jack Nicklaus demonstrates the aim of a good backswing with the shaft parallel to the target line

From a good backswing position with the shaft parallel to the target line, the club is swung back to the ball from an inside path (black arrow)

The essence of a good swing

One of the best swing thoughts on the course is to swing the clubhead on the correct path through the ball towards the target

movement. In the backward swing the large muscles of the back turn and, as the arms swing upwards, the club arrives at the top of the backswing pointing parallel to the ball to target line. From this position it is easier to swing the clubhead down on the desired inside path to the ball. But you must not rush this downward swing, since the big muscles in the thighs must be given time to initiate the downswing. As the arms start to swing down there is a gradual increase in speed due to gravity, leverage and centrifugal force. Although these terms might sound rather complicated and scientific, all three will work in your swing if you let them. Once the downswing has begun, it is like a freewheeling of the clubhead through the ball and is only stifled if you try to over-control the swing. It is important that you remember to hit through the ball and not at it, but this will happen only if your legs work correctly. Many players fail to swing through the shot because they become too ball orientated instead of thinking of the swing as a whole, or concentrating on where they want the ball to go. Once you have developed a reasonable level of hand action you should imagine that you are trying to swing the clubhead in a big circle around the axis of your spine and that the ball will just get in the way. Then you will stop over-controlling the clubhead and find yourself hitting through the ball into a well balanced finish.

The correct pace and rhythm

The professional who has mastered the individual parts of the game will feel his swing much more as a whole entity, and although he may have to work on the practice ground from time to time to correct any flaws that may occur, on the course he is most likely to think of the swing pace and rhythm, or maybe the path of the clubhead towards the target. The pace and rhythm are so important since not all of our muscles are able to move at the same speed. It is so easy for the arms and hands to swing quickly, not giving time for the bigger muscles in the back and thighs to play their part sequentially in the swing. This problem occurs because so many players are distance orientated, and believe that the faster they swing, the further the ball will go. They should remember also that the clubhead must be travelling in the right direction and from the correct angle, and that the clubface should be square at impact in order for the ball to be hit long and straight.

The club should never be swung faster than you can control it, and that will depend very much on your strength. Develop control and direction first and then you can work on creating more clubhead speed and aggression in the swing. There is a saying in golf that "if you want to hit it further, hit it better" – well worth remembering!

By finishing in a well-balanced position, you will guarantee that you have swung through the ball, and not just at it

Foot and leg action

The correct foot and leg action is often one of the last elements of the golf swing that the average player masters. Since the club is held in the hands and swung with the arms, it is usual to concentrate solely on the parts of the body directly involved in the swing and to neglect the contribution that the feet and legs must make if the arms and body are to move correctly. Golf is no different from many other sports in that the feet and legs must move in order to accommodate upper body movement and weight transference.

The correct set-up

If you set up with your feet and legs correctly positioned, then there is a good chance that they will help, rather than hinder, your swing. When you address the ball, your feet should not be too wide apart, since this will tend to restrict leg action. Neither should the stance be too narrow, or you will not provide a sufficiently stable base to the swing. As a generalization, for the driver, the inside of your heels should be about shoulder width apart, with the stance narrowing the shorter the club you use.

Weight distribution

The weight should be concentrated more on the inside of each foot rather than on the outside. With the driver, your weight should be distributed about 60/40 in favour of your right foot; with fairway shots about 50/50; and for short irons, about 60/40 in favour of your left foot. The weight should be more towards the ball of each foot. Many make the mistake of having too much weight on their heels, which prevents the feet and legs from being lively. Where the feet and legs are used actively in a sport

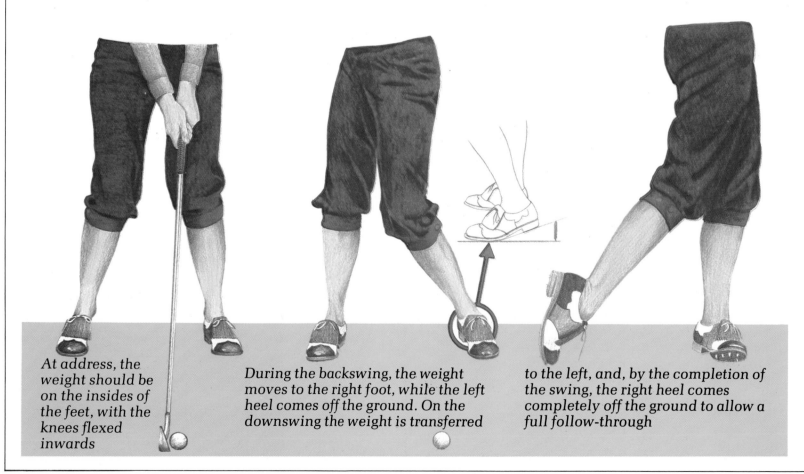

At address, the weight should be on the insides of the feet, with the knees flexed inwards

During the backswing, the weight moves to the right foot, while the left heel comes off the ground. On the downswing the weight is transferred

to the left, and, by the completion of the swing, the right heel comes completely off the ground to allow a full follow-through

the weight is always towards the balls of the feet, and golf is no exception.

Foot position

The right foot should be at right angles to the ball to target line, whereas the left foot should be turned out a little towards the target. This arrangement enables the right foot to give support in the backswing, and the left foot to permit the correct amount of freedom to the legs and hips on the throughswing. However, if you have problems making a full enough backswing, you may find it useful to turn the right foot out a little, thus allowing your hips to rotate more easily.

The knees should be flexed, and angled slightly towards each other. Tall people may find themselves having to flex their knees rather more than the shorter player, who must guard against losing height.

The backswing

As the backswing begins, you will

The fluid leg action of Tom Watson ensures that the upper body stays behind the ball as the club begins its downward path

start to feel more pressure on the inside of the right leg, and the left knee will begin to flex more. At this point, as the right leg starts to take more weight, there is a common tendency to let the knee straighten, thus releasing the pressure but ruining the chances of a good backswing. Instead, as the top of the swing is reached, there should be a considerable amount of weight on the inside of the right foot and the right leg, which should retain approximately the same amount of flex as at address. The left knee should now be pointing behind the ball, and the left heel will be raised off the ground. The question of whether the left heel should rise or not is one to which there is more than one answer. Some of the top men professionals make superb backswings leaving the left heel down, while others, such as Tom Watson, can be seen to raise it quite well off the ground. It rather depends just how flexible you are, but if the heel does come off the ground, it should be as the last movement in the backswing, and might only be slightly raised, or a couple of inches, again depending on your flexibility and the fullness of shot. You must understand that the heel leaves the ground only as a result of a full wind up, and not as an initial movement. When playing half shots, you will find that it is sufficient to roll onto the inside of the left foot rather than raise the heel.

Change of direction

From the top of the backswing, the first movement is to return the left heel to the ground, and this, in turn, moves the left knee and hip laterally towards the target. Weight is thus transferred to the inside of the left foot, and as the right leg starts to play its role in the swing, the weight moves to the outside of the left foot at impact. If, from the top of the back-

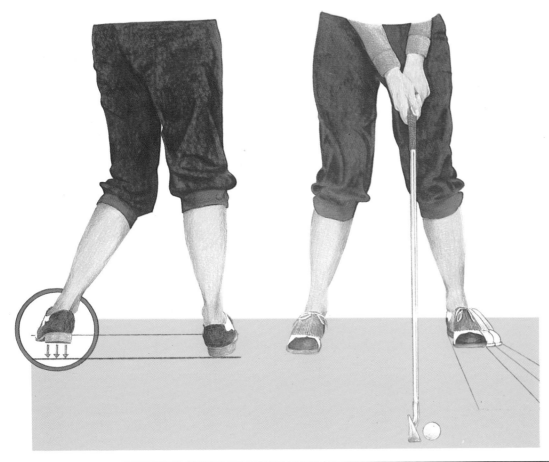

By turning the left foot out towards the target you will find it easier to clear your hips on the downswing

Foot and leg action

swing, the right, instead of the left, leg is used first, then there is a tendency for the whole of the right side to be thrown outside the correct downswing path, resulting in any number of bad shots.

Studying swing sequences of top players shows that the gap between the knees at the top of the swing widens at the start of the downswing. This can only happen if the left knee, not the right, moves first.

Impact and beyond
At impact, the left leg should have approximately the same amount of flex as it had at address, and by this time, as the right leg supplies some added power, the right heel will be starting to leave the ground. At the completion of the swing, most of the weight will move to the outside of the left heel, and the right toe will provide a stable support. Many players find it difficult to achieve this position, mainly because they do not allow the right heel to rise off the ground. Whilst some top professionals may leave the left heel on the ground at the top of the backswing, none of them will leave the right heel there on the throughswing. By permitting it to rise, you will achieve a more aggressive swing through the ball, rather than a hit at it, and also reduce the possibility of any strain on your back.

Weight transference
Correct leg action also allows the right weight transference in the golf swing. This can be likened to throwing a ball overarm, where, from a standing position, you would allow your weight to go onto your back foot and then transfer to your front foot before throwing the ball. If you are experiencing difficulties, you can learn something about how correct foot and leg action should feel, just by throwing a few stones.

Leg movement in the swing
Having learned how the feet and legs should work, they have to be co-ordinated into the swing. For the beginner, concentrating on a good arm swing is the first task, but this should not be at the expense of totally neglecting some foot and leg action. If only the top half of the body is contributing to the swing, it will be hard to maintain the correct swing path with the clubhead. From the top of the swing, instead of the left heel and leg moving first, the body will tend to heave at the ball. If you fall into this category, you would do well to practise moving the left heel and leg at the same time as you start to swing your arms down from the top of the backswing. You should also concentrate on swinging to a well balanced finish, which you can hold for a few seconds. First try this on the practice ground, where you will not be so concerned about where the ball is going. You may also find it helpful to adopt your address position, but hold a club parallel to the ground with your hands about a foot apart. From here swing back and through, and you will find that your legs respond a little more than in the golf swing.

Younger players often exhibit a very strong leg action and having learned the basics of the golf swing, they tend to copy their favourite professional, accentuating the leg action but forgetting how well the professional swings his arms. Strong leg action is useless unless the arms can match leg speed. It is pointless driving with your legs from the top of the backswing, if the clubhead is going to get left behind as this will result only in a weak fading shot.

Common faults
One of the most common faults on the backswing is to roll onto the outside of the right foot. This is usually as a result of swaying, rather than turning in the backswing. One way of curing this is to practise with a golf ball under the outside of your right foot. You will then find it impossible to roll onto the outside, and while this may feel rather restricting, it serves as a good practice aid. You would also find it helpful to hit shots from a slightly downhill lie, where your right foot is higher than the left. From this set-up it is more difficult to sway off the ball, and you will feel more pressure on the inside of your right leg at the top of the swing. Those players who straighten the right leg on the backswing would also benefit from similar practice.

If you are experiencing problems getting through the ball into a good, well balanced finish, hit some shots from a slightly uphill lie, where your left leg is higher than your right. You will have to work your legs extremely hard to get to a good finish, so that when you return to a level lie, you will find the task much easier. Practice from this sort of lie also helps if you have difficulty transferring weight to the right on the backswing.

At address(1) Curtis Strange's knees are flexed and as he starts the backswing(2) the left knee is pulled in towards the right(3). At the top of the swing(4) and the right leg has remained firm but still flexed ready to push off as he starts the downswing(5). Approaching impact(6) and the knees are sliding through towards the target with the right leg providing the drive(7) that carries him on to a balanced finish with the weight on the outside of the left foot(8)

The route to lower scores is provided by greater control of the golf ball. This control can only be attained by correct striking. Knowing why the ball exhibits different characteristics in flight is a major step in improving your control of it. It is also important to know how the loft on each club can affect the flight and control of the ball and to translate this into distance and accuracy. This chapter gives you a clear insight into these factors and provides you with a greater understanding of what happens when the clubface strikes the ball. Learn also how to use your fairway woods.

The simple approach to impact

There is an ever-increasing band of self-analysts for whom a free-flowing golf swing is something foreign simply because their minds are so cluttered up with all the things they feel they should be trying to do and positions they should be trying to achieve. This, of course, causes undue tension and tension prevents freedom and flow. If the mind is not free, neither will the swing be.

The great Australian player Peter Thomson, like all fine players, lays great emphasis on a good set-up and his own description of his swing goes something like this: "I draw the club back and then swing it forward." You cannot make it any more simple than that and it has won Thomson five Open Championships, a host of titles all over the world and tremendous success on the US Senior Tour at the age of fifty six.

It is an approach that not only engenders success but also withstands the test of time! If an aspiring young golfer was instructed by a teacher with Peter Thomson's philosophy, his grounding in the game would be simple, his mind would be free and his game, as a result, would continue to improve. He would not necessarily become the best player in the business but at least he would not complain that golf is difficult and complicated! This theme lies at the root of most of the problems of young players. A percentage of them know either little or nothing about the fundamentals of the swing and therefore have no basis from which to form a clear, simple and correct concept. The bigger percentage, usually the older ones, tend to confuse themselves and their swings by getting involved with a variety of ideas and methods – mainly gimmicks. The end product is the same frustrating ritual with the hope that the "secret" will miraculously appear at any moment!

With a clear-cut concept, practice

At impact, Sandy Lyle (left) has kept his height and swung the club into the back of the ball – back to the position from which he started. Note the minimal leg action and how both the back of the left hand and the clubface are pointing towards the target. After impact, Tom Watson is being pulled through and under by the clubhead. The club is already on its way back inside, as you will notice by the way it is beginning to look left

Three stages of Greg Norman's swing, showing how he moves through good positions instinctively. In the downswing, the left side is leading

with the lower body initiating the action. As he approaches impact, the hands have hardly moved but the clubhead has, by comparison,

travelled a great distance. At impact, the lower left side has continued its recoil, making room for the passage of the hands, arms and clubhead

becomes something to look forward to with the realization that eventually, if not immediately, everything will come right. In other words, practice will be constructive, not destructive. You will go a long way towards achieving this state if you think simply and logically about the swing. Do not complicate something that is basically a very simple and straightforward movement.

Now, staying with this simple theme, it is important that you remember this – good players *swing* the club through, bad players *take* it through.

If you watch good players, you will see positions approaching impact and after that are common to them all; positions, once again, that are purely the result of good swinging, that are *swung through*, not to.

Remember, there is no time for con-

scious manipulation on the downswing. Once your swing changes its direction, you are committed!

The main difference between good and bad players is that the good player swings the clubhead into the back of the ball and is *pulled* through and under to the finish by the momentum of the club. This produces a good, freewheeling action of the clubhead briefly down the target line before it travels back inside again. The bad player *takes* the club through or, if you like, *heaves* it through with his upper body. This produces a blocking action of the clubhead, out-to-in across the target line, and a slice, pull or top is the general result.

In a good swing, the upper body does what it is told. It is *led* both back and through by the arms swinging the clubhead. In a bad swing, the upper body dominates; it does the leading.

Most bad swings stem from various forms of interference by the player; interference, that is, with the natural free swinging action. The swing is more natural than most of you might imagine!

Interference can take many forms, but with a high percentage of players it begins at address with a bad set-up, grip or aim, and probably all three. Then, of course, swing compensations are required to make up for this, which is impossible on a repetitive basis. This is how almost everyone plays the game and is the reason they progress to a certain handicap (mainly high) and then are stuck on it. You can do yourself an enormous favour by getting rid of the interference at address and developing your grip, set-up and aim. It is at least fifty per cent of what it takes to become a consistently good player.

Keep the violence out of your swing!

It would be fair to say that most people who take an interest in swing technique know that the biggest percentage of bad shots are caused when the upper body takes charge of the downswing. That is, when instead of swinging the clubhead down and into the back of the ball with your hands and arms, you heave from the top of your backswing with your shoulders. This action throws the clubhead onto an outside track and across the ball from out-to-in. A whole variety of bad shots can be the result but mainly a slice or pull.

Why does the upper body dominate the swings of bad players? The main reason is simple – it is called the 'hit syndrome'. Most golfers either do not know or cannot fully convince themselves how far a ball will travel by just swinging the clubhead well within themselves. Instead, they feel that they must use serious physical effort in order to achieve the distance they would like. This obsession of hit and distance causes them to tighten up at address and that tightness leads to snatching the club away from the ball, a probable loss of control at the top and the inevitable heave with the upper body. Not only does this act of violence knock the club from its correct path, but it also actually retards the flow and therefore the speed of the clubhead.

On countless occasions, over-energetic pupils have been asked to swing with half the effort they felt they normally used. The look of surprise on their faces when they see the ball streaking out there as far as, if not further than, they normally hit it, and certainly straighter, is always a joy to see.

Many years ago a golfer who struggled on a 19 handicap went for a coaching lesson. He was 6ft 2in tall, weighed 14 stones and was as strong as an ox, and suffered badly from the hit syndrome. He just threw himself at the ball and carved it all over the place, but mainly with a wild slice.

He was asked whether he felt his problem was distance or direction. When he replied distance he was met with disbelief, but he still disagreed. He was challenged to a duel: his opponent used only two clubs, a 7-iron and a putter and won the match 7 and 6. He was more than a little shattered by the experience! It certainly proved the point to him, however.

His opponent suggested they play again the following week when he would use his full set and play him off his 19 handicap. In the meantime, he was told to practise swinging at half his normal pace and effort. He came along the following week, played to 10 handicap and won resoundingly! He struck the ball much further but, even more importantly, with greater accuracy. He had learned in a week to swing the clubhead and not himself.

Probably the most important statement regarding the golf action ever made was by one of the best teachers of all time, the late Ernest Jones, when he said, "You cannot move the clubhead faster than you can swing it." You should remember this every time you step up to the ball.

Programme yourself

Now another point worth noting. How often have you seen a club golfer make two or three practice swings like poetry in motion, finishing in perfect balance? Then that same player will step up to the ball and heave away, almost falling over with the effort. What is the point in making beautiful practice swings if what you do with the ball in front of you bears no resemblance? The idea of practice swings is to programme what you want to do when you actually step up to the shot.

By all means have a practice swing, but take the same feeling of ease and lightness with you to the ball and try to simulate it in the sense of tempo, degree of effort and balance. Think of the ball as being merely in the way of your clubhead and not something to be hit at.

A good swing is one whole movement from start to finish with no time for conscious manipulation on the way down. If golfers involved themselves more with feeling the clubhead and swinging it, instead of positions and various methods, they would all be better players.

Michael King is a fine swinger of the club. His relaxed set-up and smooth takeaway take him through to a well-coiled backswing from which the downswing is initiated instinctively from the lower left side. The left side leads through the downswing, with the clubhead being released automatically. He swings the clubhead down and through impact with a ball-turf contact, finishing in a well-balanced position

Improve your driving

The golfer who becomes a good driver of the ball will certainly make the rest of the game easier for himself. If you could always play the second shot from the ideal position on the fairway, the green would not seem such a difficult target to hit. Indeed, if the amateur golfer could hit the professional's drive, his handicap would soon be reduced. The professional and low handicap players become good drivers because, not only do they possess the right technique for hitting a good drive, but they also have the discipline that has to be adopted for this part of the game. This discipline is two-fold: first, that of knowing where and when to hit the driver; and secondly, that of how hard to hit the ball.

Where and when
The art of good scoring is to plot your way around the course in as few shots as possible. Nowhere is it written that on every long hole you have to hit the driver, but regardless of their ability and the hazards around, this seems to be the dictum by which many club golfers play the game. Instead, you should think about each hole before you play it and decide where you would most like to play your second shot from. In this assessment you must be realistic and not suddenly choose an area 250 yards down the fairway, when your best drive ever has only reached 220 yards. You also have to weigh up the situation regarding hazards, and whether or not they

This impact position shows why Greg Norman is one of the longest, straightest drivers in the world

It is important to plan your route at each hole in your mind before you play it. Be aware of which hazards may be in play and then choose the area from which you would like to *be hitting your next shot, and concentrate on hitting to that spot and forget about the hazards. Be realistic, and use a fairway wood or an iron if your driver is too risky*

are likely to come into play. It is pointless trying to carry a bunker or ditch that is going to need your best swing of the round, when to lay up short would only mean taking one extra club for your second shot. At this time also, it is easy to be influenced by your partners. If they are trying to carry some distant hazard regardless of the outcome, you can often just follow the trend. If the green is visible, try to see where the pin is, since if it is cut behind a bunker on the right, it would be better to approach the green from the left half of the fairway.

Decide on your game plan and stick to it, because if you change your mind, invariably you will be in two minds as you address the ball and therefore not totally committed to what you are doing. So if you have to lay up short of a hazard, take the correct club for the distance, even though it may be a fairway wood or an iron, and play the hole in the way you have mapped out in your mind.

How hard to swing

The problem with using a driver is that most players believe they are capable of infinity when it comes to distance, and therefore try to hit the ball as hard as they can. On the fairways you can be fairly disciplined in this respect, since it is always possible to take a stronger club instead of trying to thrash a 5-iron the distance you usually hit a good 4-iron. But, if you are hitting the driver and you do not have a stronger club in your bag, then the temptation may arise to try to hit it as hard as you can. The same pace and rhythm should be maintained with the driver as with the rest of the clubs; otherwise, the whole swing will tend to fall out of synchronization. It is quite obvious at times that top players like Greg Norman, who are extremely strong, hit the occasional drive extra hard, but they are well practised in making sure that the swing remains smooth and controlled, whereas the high handicap player, in an effort to achieve distance, will launch his whole body at the shot, and most probably achieve

Improve your driving

very little. It is a good idea to hit shots on the practice ground with a 6-iron and then without changing the rhythm or strength of the swing to hit the driver. Out on the course, you could try imagining that when you are using the driver, you have the 6-iron in your hand, and reproduce the rhythm and speed as for that club.

Which driver?

Many top professionals pay out a small fortune each year in an effort to find the right driver, such is the importance of the club. All too often, the high handicap player is trying to hit a club that does not suit him and will not help him to produce a respectable shot. The loft on a driver and the way the clubface sits to the ball are very important. Most club golfers should try to get a driver with about 12 degrees loft or possibly more. The less loft a club has, the more sidespin it will produce, and as most club golfers' swings put too much sidespin on the ball, you want a club that will tend to offset this effect. However, many drivers have only about 10 degrees or less, so this may mean that the right club in your set for you to drive with is in fact the 3-wood, since this has more loft than the driver. For the beginner, a 4- or 5-wood would be suitable, since the additional loft in these clubs will help the player even more, and he will gain confidence from hitting the ball reasonably straight, if not very far. You should check also that the clubface sits square to the line of flight at address as this, unfortunately, is not always the case. Some players use the name transfer at the top of the club as a lin-

ing-up guide, but you must make sure that this is put on absolutely square, or it is a useless aid.

The swing

The correct in-to-in swing for a driver produces a fairly shallow angle of attack, so that the ball can be swept off the tee peg at the bottom of the swing or even slightly on the way up. To achieve this action the ball should be teed up so that the back of the ball is about two inches inside the left heel. This position does vary from player to player, so a little experimentation may be needed, but the ball should be positioned opposite the point where the clubhead is just on the way up. There should be slightly more weight on the right foot than the left, and the

With the ball positioned just inside the left heel, Corey Pavin (left) keeps the clubhead low and wide at the start of the backswing. At the top of the backswing, Ben Crenshaw's shoulders have turned 90 degrees, and his left heel has risen as his weight is transferred to his right side

shoulders should be square. This is often where the problem arises, since, as the ball is at its most forward position in the game, it is easy for the shoulder line to get open to the target. This in turn is likely to produce a steep out-to-in swing, which is just what you are trying to avoid, so check the ball position and your shoulder line if your driving is erratic. From the set-up, as the arms swing back, the

As Andy Bean (left) accelerates through the ball, his head eventually rotates towards the target, maintaining the original spinal angle. At the completion of his swing, Johnny Miller is perfectly balanced, with most of his weight on the outside of his left foot and his right heel completely off the ground

clubhead must be kept fairly low to the ground for about the first 18 inches and the hands must not pick the clubhead up too steeply. At the same time, the body must start to turn to provide width to the swing, so that at the top of the backswing, most of the weight is on the right leg, and the shoulders are turned approximately 90 degrees. With the driver, you will be more aware of your body turn, and may feel some slight tension across the back muscles as they are stretched into action. From the top, as the arms swing the clubhead down from inside the ball to target line, weight is transferred to the left side and the hips start to clear, so that the arms have room to swing through, past the ball into a well-balanced finish. Hitting at the ball must be avoided; instead, concentrate on swinging through to the finish, so that most of your weight is on your left leg, your right heel is off the ground, and you are facing straight down the fairway. Do not keep your head down for too long after you have hit the ball as this will inhibit a good throughswing. Instead, allow it to rotate towards your target but maintain the same spinal axis as at impact.

Where and how to tee the ball

Lining-up is crucial with the driver since, as you hit a drive further than any other shot, if it is hit off line it will go further off line. So always pick an intermediate target about two to three feet ahead of the ball as a guide and aim over that. Since the tee shot is the one time you can choose where to hit from, make certain that you pick a flat and even part of the tee. Some clubs seem to leave the tee boxes in the same position for far too long, resulting in that particular area becoming very worn and uneven. In such instances, it is worthwhile teeing up slightly behind the tee boxes, so that you get an even stance on an unworn area. If the ball is teed at the correct height, the centre should be level with the top edge of the club, so obviously this varies according to the depth of the clubface. You should also check which is the preferable side of the tee from which to hit, since this may help with the direction of the shot. If there is an out of bounds or some such similar hazard down the left-hand side of the fairway, tee up on the left side of the tee. From this position it will be easier to aim away from the trouble than if you were to stand on the right side.

Summary

Be aware of when and where you should use your driver, plan your route on each hole and use the correct club accordingly. Swing with the same pace and rhythm with the driver as the irons. Check that your driver is suitable for your standard of golf – the more loft, the easier it is to hit. Do not be too proud to use fairway woods from the tee if you hit them better. Be selective on where you tee up and always aim away from hazards. Keep the swing wide by keeping the clubhead low to the ground initially, and swing through the shot – do not hit at the ball.

Know your distance

Once you have started to hit the ball more consistently, it is important to be able to judge two aspects connected with distance: first, how far you can hit each club and, secondly, how far to your target. It is all too easy, when playing with friends, to see which number club they are using, and then just to use the same one. But golf does not work like that, and it is important for you to play your own game. In order to do so, you must work out how far you hit each club.

How far do you hit each club?
Preferably on a calm day, go to the practice ground, select a flat area and hit about 20 shots with, say, a 9-iron. You should pace off to the centre of where the group of balls has landed, ignoring the one or two you may have totally mishit, and also those that may have flown well past the main cluster. You will then know how many paces you can hit your 9-iron. Repeat this procedure with the rest of your clubs, and then you will have a table to which you can relate. You could, of course, just do the odd numbered clubs, and work out the rest from there, but in hitting each club in progression, you should also discover if the lofts on your clubs are reasonably correct. There should be a difference in length of about 10 yards per club. When hitting the wedge and sand wedge, do guard against trying to hit them too hard – these clubs are made for accuracy and feel, not for distance. So assess their yardage from what feels to you like a three-quarter swing.

Pacing the course
The golfer who tends to play mainly on his home course gets to know which club he hits from certain landmarks, so that distance becomes the most difficult thing to judge when he visits another course. In order to rectify this, it would be a good idea to pace your home course – naturally at a time when few people are playing. You should pace off the distance to any bunkers that you could drive into from the tee, together with the safe distance to lay up to them and also to carry them. The same should be done for any cross ditches on your course. Then pick a permanent landmark, such as a bunker or tree, and pace from there to the front of the green. If it is a long hole you will need to take a yardage from another point along the fairway to help you judge the distance of your third shot. Now pace the depth of the green and you may be surprised just how long some greens can be – as much as 40 yards on some courses, which from the guidelines above could mean a difference of four clubs from front to back. At this point, it would serve you well to note what is over the back of the green. Most golf shots end up short of the pin, sometimes because of mishits, but more often due to wrong club

selection. If you know that it is trouble-free beyond the green, you may be encouraged to take the right club more often. Also most greenside bunkers tend to be placed at the front of the green, so that is another reason to make sure that your shot in is long enough. Whereas you will probably know where the worst spots are on your own course, you should check on each hole when you are playing on another course – whether there are definite areas to avoid, such as out of bounds or ponds. That way, you will be able to plan your route to the hole to your best advantage.

So start with pacing your home club, and that will help you to convert unknown distances into yards, or paces, and, together with your knowledge of how far you hit each club, this will improve your golf not only at home but on other courses, too. Although you may not be able always to pace off the courses you visit, you can always step it off from the tee, so

The correct club to hit the ball to the middle of a green level with the fairway will only reach the front of an elevated green, but the back of a green lower than the fairway

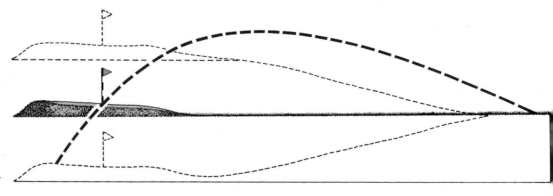

*By knowing the depth of the green,
and where the problem areas are,
you will be better able to select the
right club for the shot in hand*

that you know how many yards are left to the hole. With more clubs providing ready-made yardage charts of their course, many golfers are starting to appreciate how knowing the distance can help their round and the good club golfer can benefit nearly as much as the professional.

Club selection

Knowing the distance you have to hit the ball should be regarded purely as a starting point in club selection. Other elements, such as the lie of the ball, wind direction and strength, and pin position, also have to be taken into consideration. If the ball is sitting well, then club selection is not affected, but if it is lying in a hole, or thick rough, you may have to compromise, and this is the time that lay-up yardage is so important. If the ball is on an uphill lie it will fly higher, so you need a stronger club. If it is on a downhill lie, it will fly lower, and you can use a weaker club. You must also make allowances for shots where the green is on a different level to the ball. If the green is elevated, you must take more club if you do not want to be short; whereas to a green below you, a more lofted club can be used. From a position where the ball is above your feet, it will hook and tend to go further, but if it is below them, it will tend to slice and therefore not travel so far.

Wind direction and strength can change very quickly on a golf course, where some shots may be protected by the trees, and others open to the full force of a gale. The wind may be blowing in one direction where you are standing, and another by the green, so take a good look at which

way the flag is flying. Obviously downwind you will need less club, and more into the wind, but just how much you should allow for the wind will depend on its strength. Cross winds will also reduce the length of the shot, as well as affect the direction so, again, take a less lofted club. A general rule for playing in the wind is to take more club when necessary and never try to hit the ball harder, but use a controlled swing.

Pin position should also affect your choice of club. Whereas most players might be happy just to hit the middle of the green, you will score better, and set up more birdie chances, the closer you put the ball to the hole. So if the pin looks to be either very close to the front or back of a long green, choose

your club accordingly. On a two-tiered green, it may make a big difference to your score if you can get the ball on the same tier as the pin. One instance where you will want to be short of the hole with your approach is on a sharply uphill green, where you would benefit by leaving yourself an uphill, rather than a downhill, first putt.

The ability to judge distances by eye is a great asset which can work very well for you, but this can often be hindered by pins of varying sizes on a course, tending to distort length. Long pins foreshorten the distance, whereas particularly short ones do the opposite. For the more competitive golfer, learning something about how far you hit the ball and the distance you have to cover, can save many shots per round, but do all your pacing and calculating in a brisk manner, or you may find yourself short of partners.

Know the laws of ball flight

Successful golf is a result of ball control rather than 'swings' of which there have been many successful, but very different, ones. If we accept this basic concept regarding ball control, then what the clubhead is doing when it hits the ball is the determining factor above all else. The key factors at impact are: clubhead speed, clubface alignment, the swing path and the actual angle of approach to the ball.

Ideally, we would like an impact with maximum clubhead speed with the clubface square and the swing path on line with the club reaching the ball at the appropriate angle of attack. When this is not the case, the ball itself is the best indicator as to what has gone wrong. However, when all is said and done, the ball can start only left or right of the desired line which indicates the swing path. It can curve only left or right in the air, which indicates clubface alignment relative to the swing path. Ball trajectory gives a clear indication of the angle of approach of the club to the ball – a shallow arc through the ball will fly it relatively low whereas a steep, narrow arc tends to fly the ball much higher.

An open stance may often lead to a flat backswing (1). A ball starting left then curving left has been hit from out-to-in with a closed clubface (2). A ball going straight left has been hit from out-to-in with the clubface square to that line (3). A ball starting left then curving right has been hit from out-to-in with the clubface open to that line (4)

One of the difficulties of playing golf is that many players are often not achieving what they think they are doing. A simple illustration of this is when the ball finishes to the left and most golfers assume that they have hit out-to-in. However, a quick look at the divot may show that the swing path was straight or even to the right of target. This confirms that the ball has gone to the left because of a closed clubface. In fact, the clubface is quite the most important factor of the impact dimension since if this one is wrong, the swing path and, therefore, the angle of approach of the club to

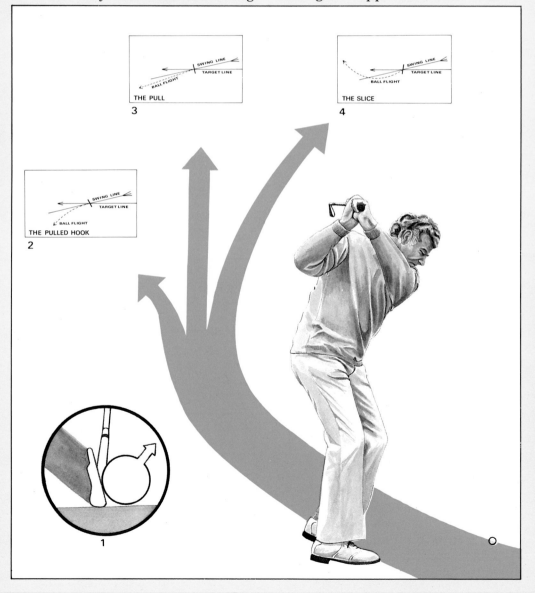

THE PULL

3

THE SLICE

4

THE PULLED HOOK

2

1

It is important to understand how the loft of the club affects the spin on the ball. The straight-faced clubs, which make contact near the centre of the back of the ball, impart side-spin (right). Lofted clubs hit the bottom of the ball, which causes backspin rather than side-spin (far right), even when the clubface is open

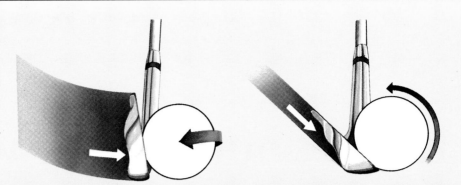

the ball will quickly follow suit.

If the clubface is making contact with the ball in an open position, the vast majority of players will automatically swing out-to-in. This leads to a too-steep angle of approach of the club since fear of going to the right will dominate. Conversely, if the clubface is closed at impact the swing path will automatically become in-to-out which actually leads to the bottom of the arc being behind the ball and thus an upward blow being delivered.

The out-to-in, open clubface, steep angle of attack will work reasonably well with the pitching clubs but not with the straight-faced ones. The closed clubface and in-to-out upward attack very often drives the ball quite well if sufficient loft is used on the club, but the pitching clubs will suffer since the necessary ball-turf contact is unobtainable.

One further aspect that needs to be mentioned and understood is how the loft on the club affects the spin applied to the ball. It is only relatively straight-faced clubs, which make contact near the centre of the back of the ball, that can impart side-spin. Therefore, the straight-faced clubs give the best indication of the club-face position at impact. The lofted clubs obviously strike the bottom of the golf ball and, therefore, impart backspin as opposed to side-spin, even when the clubface is open.

It follows, therefore, that an out-to-in impact with the clubface open will create a left to right slice with the straight-faced clubs, such as a driver or long iron, but will tend to pull shots straight to the left with the pitching clubs since, in this instance, backspin will be predominant. This explains why so many golfers slice their long shots and pull the short ones. It is important to make an effort to understand your own ball flight in terms of the impact since this understanding is the real step to lasting improvement in your game.

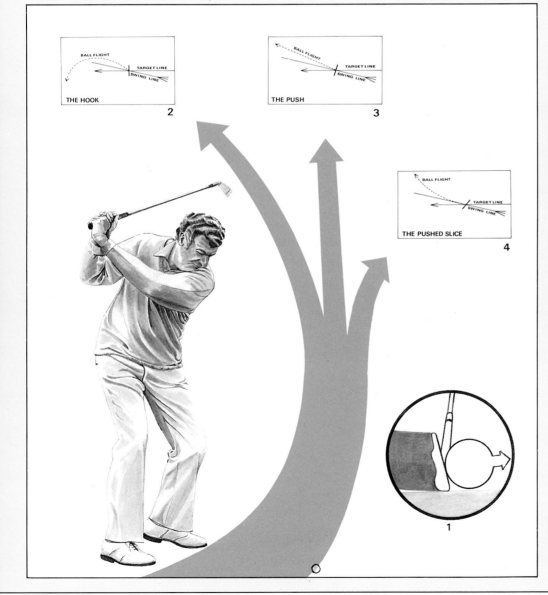

BALL FLIGHT
TARGET LINE
SWING LINE
THE HOOK
2

BALL FLIGHT
TARGET LINE
SWING LINE
THE PUSH
3

BALL FLIGHT
TARGET LINE
SWING LINE
THE PUSHED SLICE
4

1

A closed stance produces a relatively shallow angle of approach and a low trajectory shot(1). As before, the flight of the ball will tell you how the clubface was at impact

Know your fairway woods

The group of players that finds taking a divot with their iron clubs rather difficult will probably prefer using wooden clubs. An iron shot requires descending swing, striking the ball first and then taking a divot. However, with a wooden club, the swing is shallower, and therefore the clubhead skims across the top of the grass and no divot is taken. Consequently, the player who has a swing that is perhaps a little flat, or who does not have sufficient strength to strike through the turf, will enjoy hitting woods. Psychologically, the larger head of a fairway wood always looks more inviting to use than the smaller head on, say, a 2- or 3-iron, and whereas one would expect to hit a 5-wood and a 2-iron about the same distance, the extra loft on the wood, 25 degrees compared to 19, makes it a more forgiving club.

Ball position and set-up
To ensure that the ball is swept away, the clubhead must make contact when it is at the bottom of its arc, and the ball should be positioned therefore to coincide with that point – about one to one-and-a-half inches nearer your left foot than for an iron shot. When you address the ball, bend slightly from the hips to give your arms room to swing. Your weight should be divided equally between both feet, but should you encounter a very good lie, where the ball is sitting on a small tuft of grass, you could put a little more weight on the right leg, so that you can be certain of sweeping the shot away. Make sure that the clubhead is sitting flat on the ground. Many players hood the club at address, i.e. they get their hands too far ahead of the ball, thus raising the back edge of the club and changing the effective loft. This also encourages too steep a swing.

The swing
With a wood, it is important to create a wide, shallow swing, and therefore you must ensure that as your arms swing the club back, your body turns sufficiently. If you just lift your arms in the backswing, you will create a chopping action on the ball – not what you want with a fairway wood. If you make the correct turn, you will

With the ball positioned about 1-1½ inches nearer your left foot than for iron shots, swing the clubhead back wide and low, so that you attack the ball from a shallow angle. If you have too steep a swing, similar to that of an iron, your shots will tend to be struck erratically

Iron

Fairway Wood

feel your back muscles working harder with the longer clubs than with the shorter ones. You must also make certain that you allow your weight to transfer to the right leg in the backswing, even if it means that you feel your head has moved a little to allow for this. You should guard against having too much weight on your left foot at the top of the backswing, which will encourage too steep an attack on the ball and this is the very thing you are trying to avoid. As you swing your arms down, you should concentrate on sweeping the ball from the turf and keeping all thoughts of hitting down on the shot from your mind. Hit well through the ball – do not swing at it.

Which wood to use

Most sets of clubs nowadays come with a driver, 3-wood, and 5-wood, but the lofts on these clubs can vary a little between manufacturers. Most 3-woods have about 16 degrees loft, whereas a 5-wood has 25. The 3-wood is ideal from the fairway if you have a good lie, and also in the rough if the ball is sitting up. However, the 5-wood is the more versatile club for as well as using it on the fairway from good lies, you can make a few alterations to the set-up and swing and use it from a less than perfect situation, even from the rough. If the ball is sitting down, e.g. in a shallow divot, you must use the wood a bit more like an iron – position the ball where you would for an iron and keep your hands slightly more ahead of the club. Do not worry if the back edge comes off the ground. From this set-up you can make a steeper swing and dig the

Lee Trevino, with his unorthodox but highly effective swing, is master of the fairway woods

ball out of the ground, this time taking a small divot. You should use this same set-up and swing from the rough and semi-rough. The more proficient player will also be able to manoeuvre the 5-wood quite easily, and will find that by gripping down the shaft, which will alter the distance the ball will travel, the variety of shots possible increases making this a valuable club to have in the bag.

If you are lucky enough to find the ball sitting up in a shallow fairway bunker, you may be able to hit the 5-wood as long as the face is not steep. Make sure you work your feet into the sand, but not too deep, and grip down the shaft by the same amount. Position the ball as you would for a normal shot, and focus more towards the top of the ball than the back, as this will help you to take it cleanly from the top of the sand.

When using a fairway wood, you should have a mental image of sweeping the ball off the grass

Know your fairway woods

When the ball is in a divot or bad lie, a small-headed fairway wood will suit the situation better than a long-bladed iron. Play the ball nearer the centre of your stance, keeping your hands well ahead of the clubface, so that the sole of the club no longer sits flat on the turf. From this set-up, the club will be swung on a steeper plane, so that you can hit down on the ball, taking a small divot in the process

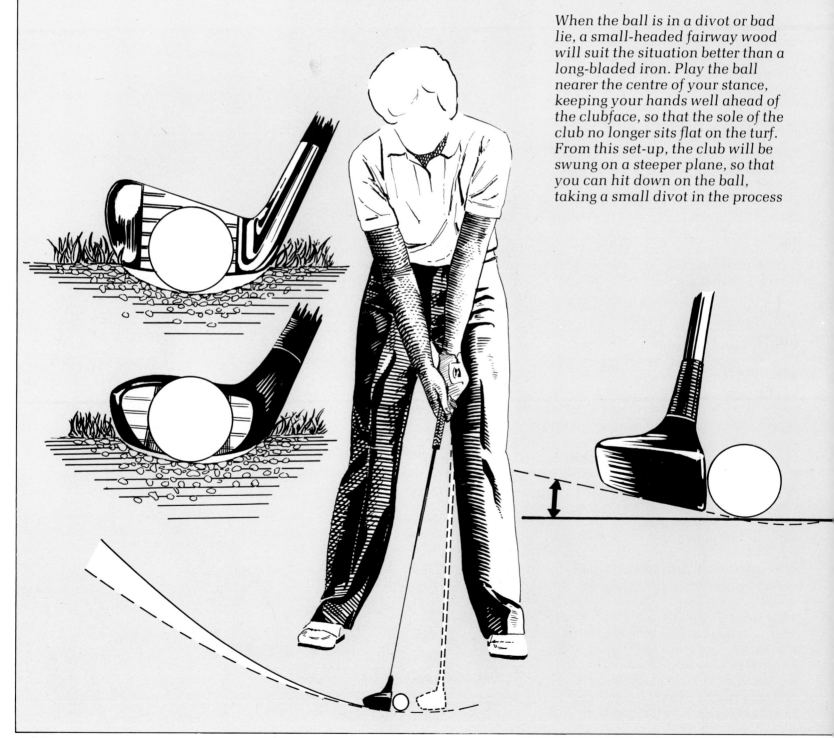

Playing in the wind

A long shot played in a strong down-wind may be more effective with a 4- or 5-wood than a 2-iron, since the extra height you would get would enable the wind to carry the ball further. Playing into the wind is a different matter. If the lie is good, you will be able to use the 3- or 4-wood, but a 5-wood may go too high, and be affected adversely. When playing into the wind, you can minimize its effect by swinging easy, restricting wrist action to a certain degree, or by putting the ball back in the stance, all of which reduces the club's loft and makes punching the ball low much easier.

Those players who prefer woods to irons may find it useful to experiment with the higher numbered woods that are now being made. For instance, Lee Trevino uses his 7-wood most effectively, and you may find such a club a useful addition to your set.

Johnny Miller (top) in a classic position with a fairway wood, note how his head remains over the ball. Bernard Hunt (right) plays a fairway wood from a poor lie: for this shot the ball should be positioned further back in the stance. David Graham (far right) shows how the club is kept on line through the ball

Chapter 4 THE SHORT GAME

No matter how good your long game is, there will be occasions when you have to rely on your short game to save par. Remember that a delicately executed chip or a long putt holed counts as much as a booming drive. Since a golfer uses the short irons more than the clubs designed for longer hitting, it stands to reason that the more accomplished you are with these clubs, the lower your scores will be. Furthermore, par allows you to take two putts on every green so the putter is by far the most used club in the bag. In this chapter you can learn how to execute those stroke-saving short shots, how to recover from bunkers and how to hole more putts. By adapting these techniques into your game, you can quickly lower your scores and thus improve your game.

The secret of perfect chipping

Although the chip shot from around the green ought to be one of the easiest to play, many beginners still come to grief with what is one of the simplest of shots. The most common fault is that the player wants to scoop the ball into the air and therefore uses a lot of independent hand action. He combines this with a set-up where the weight is too evenly distributed on each foot and the ball is too far forward. The result of all this is usually a thinned shot, which scurries across the green, only to present the player with the same shot from a different position. The easiest way for the club golfer to tackle chipping is to imagine that he is putting with an iron instead of a putter, although the set-up, and consequently the type of strike, is somewhat different.

The set-up
If you are going to improve your short game you may as well work on the direction of the shot as well as the strike, so to help with this, stand behind the ball and pick out an intermediate spot about a yard ahead on the ball to target line. Next set the bottom edge of the club square to the target, and take up your stance with the ball positioned about three inches inside your left heel. Your feet should be open, about six to eight inches apart, and turned slightly towards your target. You should place your hands lower down on the grip, which will allow for more feel and control in the shot, and your arms should be relaxed. Your hands must be ahead of the ball at address, which will take some loft off the face of the club, so a 7-iron will look more like a 6-iron. The weight should be about 60/40 in favour of the left foot, and this, together with the correct ball and hand position, will enable you to deliver the clubhead in a slightly downward direction, thus lofting the ball in the air and letting it roll to the hole. Although the feet are open, the shoulders must still be square, or otherwise the direction of the shot will be difficult to control.

The swing
The club is swung back mainly with the forearms, so there is very little hand movement and the clubhead stays fairly low to the ground. On the way through the shot, the right knee might ease towards the target, but the prime movers in the chip shot are the forearms. At impact, and well into the throughswing, the hands will be ahead of the clubface. The main error is made by the player who, at impact, stops the left hand, while the right one continues through producing either the thin or fluffed shot. One way to cure this is to keep the grip end of the club moving towards the target and then the right hand cannot become too dominant. Some players like to feel that they are using a right-handed underarm action to chip, which is acceptable provided that you keep the left hand moving as well. However, if you are having problems with acquiring a consistent contact in chipping, you should think of it more as a left-handed shot. How hard you should hit the ball will vary depending on the situation and club selection, but once you can make consistent contact, you will be better able to develop a sense of pace. Always have a couple of practice swings before the actual shot, trying to visualize where you want the ball to land. This will programme your muscles and give you an idea of how long the backswing should be. Two common faults to avoid are taking the club back too far, then slowing down into the swing, and not taking the club back far enough, causing you to use your hands at the last minute for extra power. Accelerate smoothly through the shot, trying to make the backswing and throughswing the same length.

Tom Watson (left) shows why firmness through the shot is vital for successful chipping. The relaxed position of Severiano Ballesteros (above) is the key to his mastery of the shorter shots

Club selection

The general rule for club selection is to pick the club that will loft the ball just onto the green, then let it roll towards the hole. So the first thing to understand is how the ball reacts with different clubs. A 7-iron shot will be in the air about one-third of its journey, and two-thirds on the ground. A 9-iron will be about 50/50, whereas a wedge shot will travel about two-thirds in the air, and roll one-third. So, depending on the ball's situation, you should select the right club for the job and, using the same action, let the loft of the club determine the shape of the shot. You can chip with almost any iron, but most good players use from 5- to sand irons. One way to appreciate just how the ball reacts with different clubs is to take a few balls to the chipping green, and from about two yards off

The secret of perfect chipping

the green, use each of the clubs from 5- to sand wedge in turn, applying the same amount of force to each swing. The 5-iron will go the furthest, rolling most of the way, whereas the sand iron will rise quickly into the air, settle down quite readily on landing, and travel the shortest distance. From this exercise, it will become clearer as to which club to use in each situation. If you are just off the green, and the pin is 20 yards away, a 5- or 6-iron would be ideal, but if you are 15 yards off the green, with the pin in the same position, you could use a 9-iron, landing the ball safely on the green, then letting it roll. If the pin is on the top level of a two-tier green, a 5-iron would be appropriate, as it will roll up the slope to the top level, but if the hole is cut only four or five yards onto the green, a wedge or sand iron would be the club to use. The variations are endless, but very often a more experienced player will start to favour certain clubs, using them regularly and thus they will become more familiar to his sense of feel.

Bad lies
You are not going to be fortunate enough to encounter only good lies around the green. Many areas become quite worn, especially if they are en route to the next hole. The way to cope with bad lies is to put the ball back in your stance, more towards your right foot, or even opposite it in difficult circumstances. This sets your hands well ahead of the clubface and allows an even more downward attack on the ball. Where the ball is in a divot or depression, you may have to break your wrists a little in the

backswing, so that you can get the club up steeply and quickly to hit down sufficiently. Having put the ball back, you have taken extra loft off the club, so now a 7-iron would react more like a 5-iron. You may find therefore that the wedge and sand wedge become the more useful clubs from bad lies, as their built-in loft will help to control the ball more.

Very good lies
When the ball is lying very well, perhaps on a tuft of grass, you can afford to position it a little further for-ward in your stance than for a standard shot. Still keeping your hands ahead of the clubface, sweep the ball from the grass, rather than hit down on it. The ball may go a little higher and roll less, as the club will have more effective loft on it.

Summary
Regard chipping as two forwards and one back, i.e. weight and hands forwards and the ball back. Use the right club for the shot and your forearms to swing the club back and through the same distance.

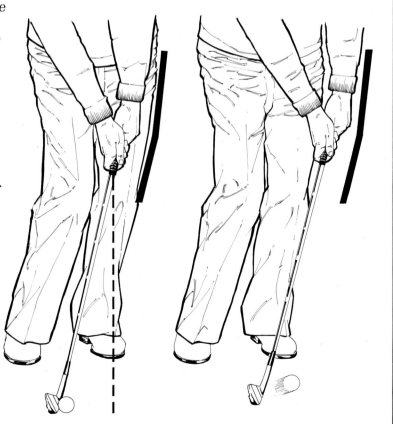

At address (right), the ball should be positioned 3-4 inches inside the left heel. The hands are ahead of the clubface, and the weight favours the left foot. Impact position should mirror the address position. To avoid the left wrist collapsing at impact, think of keeping the whole of the grip moving towards the target

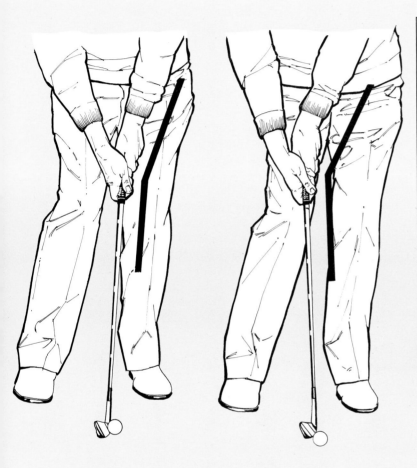

When faced with a short chip from the edge of the green, choose a club with just enough loft to carry the ball onto the putting surface

The correct set-up and ball position will enable you to hit down slightly on the ball

In the most common bad set-up, the ball is too far forward, the weight too even on both feet, and the hand too far back. This set-up encourages an incorrect impact position, where the left wrist collapses, the clubhead is swinging up instead of down, and the ball is therefore mishit

The up and over chip

This is the short game shot that most high handicap golfers fear, and that in itself is enough to prevent them from playing it successfully. Because their technique has not allowed them to produce the right type of swing for this shot, they have experienced very few satisfying results. Consequently they come to expect failure, and very often in golf we get what we expect. Many players faced with the prospect of having to pitch the ball over a bunker to a pin cut close to it rush up to the shot, quickly grab a club from their bag and make a hurried wristy jab at the ball. The result is either a fat shot, where the ball either dribbles into the bunker or stops just short of it, in which case you have the same shot to play again; or a thin shot, which may bury the ball in the bunker face, or charge across the green and off the other side.

In learning to play this shot correctly, it is important to be realistic about it. If your results and actions fit into any of the above categories, your first target has to be to learn a fairly basic action that, after a little practice, will get you over the bunker and onto the green. You may not land up very near the pin, but at least you will be putting and not still pitching or playing from a bunker.

Club selection and set-up
Club selection and set-up are all important. Since you are trying to get the ball into the air, it makes sense to use the most lofted clubs, i.e. wedge or sand wedge. If the pin is cut very close to the bunker the sand wedge would be ideal, but if you have more green with which to work, the wedge might be the club you choose. The only point to consider when using the sand wedge is the lie of the ball. Because this has a flange, which sits lower than the leading edge, there must be a cushion of grass under the ball so that the club can slide under it. Should you try to use this club from a hard bare lie, the flange will bounce off the ground and you will thin the shot. So when the ball is on a bare or tight lie, the shot would be easier with the wedge, which has no flange.

It is important to match arm swing and leg action in order to produce a fluid swing. Try to keep your knees, hands and arms moving together throughout the shot

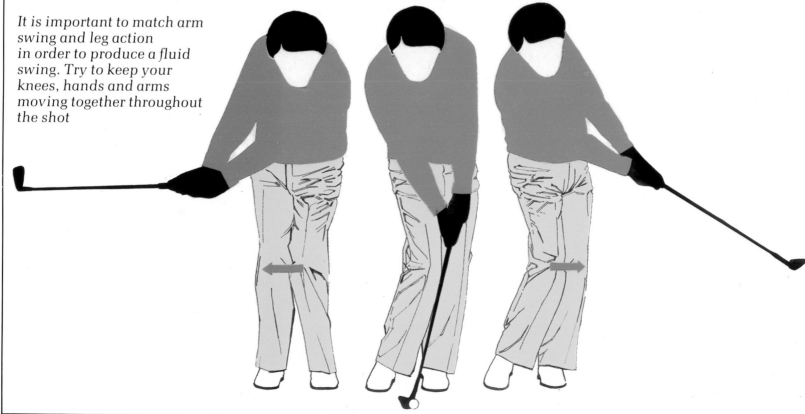

Sliding the blade of the club under the ball has enabled Bernhard Langer to execute a soft-landing recovery shot from heavy rough

Having selected the right club, you should position the ball in the middle of your stance. Your feet should still be quite close together and angled a little towards your target, but you should keep your shoulders square. Your weight will be distributed evenly on both feet. As the ball is slightly further forward in your stance than for a chip shot, your hands will not be so far ahead of it, and the shaft will be more upright as you look down at it. With your arms relaxed rather than straight, grip down the club, so that your left hand is about two or three inches from the top. The main errors to avoid in setting up to this shot are having the ball either too far forward in an effort to try to scoop it into the air, or too far back, which tends to make it fly too low.

The swing

This is primarily an arm and leg, rather than a hand, shot. You do not have to pick the club up abruptly in the backswing using a wristy action to get the ball into the air. If you swing your arms back and up, and at the same time transfer your weight to the right leg, your hands will work sufficiently without any conscious effort. As you swing through, transfer your weight to your left leg and keep your left arm moving. Your right arm must not rotate over the left, which would close the clubface. If the back of the left hand keeps going towards the target, this should not happen. Again, as with the chip shot, the right arm can become too dominant, causing the back of the left wrist to collapse at impact and ruining any chance of a good shot. Failure to transfer your

The up and over chip

weight to the left foot will produce the same error, so do not be afraid to get your legs working throughout the shot. Your set-up and swing should produce a slightly descending action on the ball, which will loft it over the bunker.

Putting the swing to work

The basic shot should be practised first using the correct set-up and swing. If your course does not have a practice bunker, you could try pitching the ball over your bag and trolley, or hit shots imagining yourself on the course and playing over one of the bunkers. Once you become a little more confident about the shot, you will approach it in a different frame of mind on the course. The next time you have to play one, first check to see just how much green you have to

work with. Very often the pin looks much closer to the bunker than it really is when you stand at the ball. Be realistic about your chances, and if the pin is cut close to the bunker do not try to be too clever. Just make sure that you loft the ball at least three or four yards over the bunker, rather than one foot, in an effort to get close. Often by viewing the shot from the side, it is easier to imagine the ball in flight and where it will land.

From this viewpoint you can also start to sense how hard it must be hit. Check your lie so you will know how the ball is likely to react. If it is sitting well up on the grass, it will fly higher than if the lie is a bit tight, thus affecting your choice of club. Have two or three practice swings, feeling how hard you need to hit the ball and visualizing it landing on the right area, and running up to the hole. Now reproduce your practice swing at the ball — be positive and you will get a good result. Try to make your practice swing exactly how the real one should be. Guard against taking too short a backswing, which will cause you to use your hands at the last moment to gain extra distance. Do not take too long a backswing and then slow down into the shot. The further you have to go, the more you must swing your arms and use your legs. When practising, find out how short a distance you can hit with both your wedge and sand irons. You will be able to vary this to some degree, not only by how far back you swing but also by how much you grip down the club. But however short the shot, always keep your legs and arms swinging to minimize hand action.

Keep the back of the left hand firm and moving throughout the shot. If the left hand stops at impact, the wrist will collapse and cause the bottom edge of the blade to contact the ball

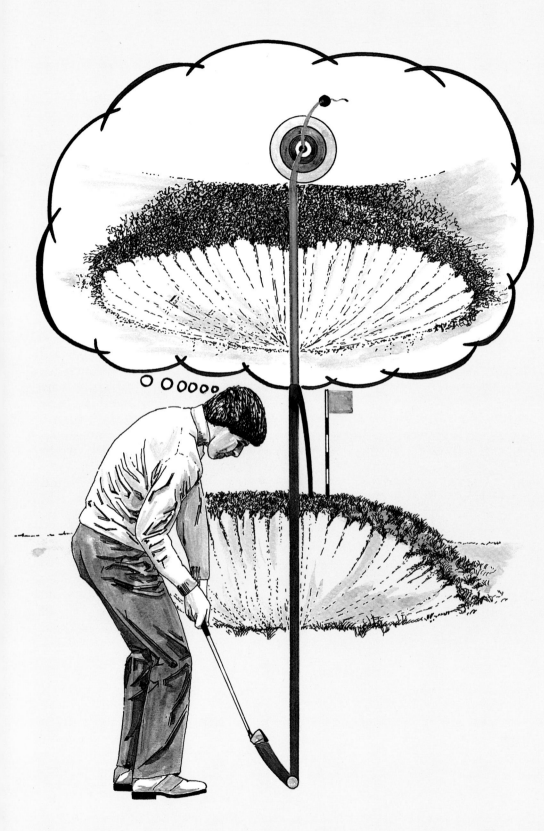

Have two or three practice swings: feel how hard you need to hit the ball and visualize it landing on the right spot, and running up to the hole. Step up to the ball and reproduce your practice swing

The more advanced shots

Once you can play the basic shot fairly successfully, you can progress to more advanced shots, which will offer more variety to your game. Using the same set-up as for the basic shot, swing your arms more steeply in the backswing to produce a shot that flies higher and therefore does not roll so far. If beginners are told to swing the club more steeply, they usually just break their wrists, producing the very action we do not want. But the more advanced player who has overcome this tendency will not fall into that trap. As the arms are swung more steeply, the wrists will break more. However, you should not try consciously to produce this. You can then experiment with opening the clubface at address, aiming left of your target, and swinging across the ball to target line. This will produce a high lob shot, but note again that it is an arm swing. By this stage you will also be able to play a shot where the arms can swing very slowly without the hands intervening. The only time you may have to cock your wrists quickly in the backswing is when you are playing out of rough and do not want the clubhead to get tangled up in the thick grass.

Summary

From the correct set-up, always swing your arms and move your legs to play the shot. Visualize where you want the ball to land and, with this in mind, produce an arm-orientated swing without conscious wrist action, allowing the club's loft to get the ball in the air. Keep the swing smooth and the back of the left hand moving throughout the shot.

Mastering the long pitch

The long pitch is probably one of the easiest shots in the short game, since it is played more often at full pace, and therefore requires less of the finesse that is needed for the delicate pitch over a bunker. A shot that can be described as a long pitch will vary according to how far you hit the ball, and the club you use, but for the club golfer it could be from a range of 65 to 120 yards. The characteristics of the shot can vary as well, from one that has a lowish penetrating flight (useful into the wind), a normal trajectory shot, or one that flies especially high. It is often the shot that you see the professionals spin backwards on landing – Greg Norman, for example, is a great exponent of this particular skill.

If you are able to play this shot well it can be a real shot saver. Many high handicap players will spend hours practising their long game, but if they spent half their time working on all departments of the short game, they would easily reduce their score by four or five shots per round. It is also very satisfying for the better players to be able to score well when their long game may be letting them down, and nothing upsets an opponent more than seeing you continually pitching the ball in close to the hole from uncharted parts of the course. To that end, some time spent on practice pitching will be very worthwhile. Some clubs are lucky enough to have a large practice ground, but even those that do not have this facility usually have a small area where you can chip or pitch so that almost everyone has the opportunity to work on the short game.

The standard pitch

To play a standard trajectory pitch shot, the ball must be positioned about three inches inside the left heel, with the feet fairly close together. Both feet and knees should be angled slightly towards the target, in order to provide resistance in the backswing and to encourage a steep swing. Your weight is on the inside of the right foot and towards the outside of the left. The club shaft is sloping towards

Bernhard Langer shows the importance of the left arm driving through into a firm, controlled position beyond impact

the target, which means the hands are ahead of the ball. While the feet and hips are open to the line of flight, the shoulders are kept square, as the swing path on this shot is from inside to straight through. As the arms and hands swing the club back and up, the shoulders turn as well, but less obviously than for long shots.

Many high handicap players feel that any pitch must be played solely with the hands, but this is not so. In this particular shot, the player will feel his wrists cock more noticeably, but this is due to the arms being swung in a steeper manner. Some weight will transfer to the inside of

Any tendency to 'scoop' the ball into the air will close the clubface prior to impact and result in hitting the ground behind the ball (right). Concentrate on hitting down into the back of the ball and let the loft of the club propel the ball upwards (far right)

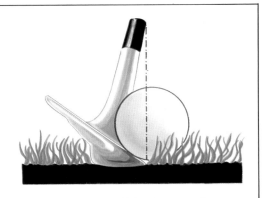

Set-up to the shot with the ball well towards your right foot, most weight on your left foot and your hands ahead of the ball. This allows you to attack the ball first and take a divot second

the right foot and then, as the arms swing down, the weight will move back to the left side. The shot is played with an abbreviated follow-through in quite a punchy but smooth manner, so that hitting down on the shot becomes the main aim in the downswing, rather than thinking about a follow-through.

While the hands are active at impact, the left hand and arm must be strong through the impact area to prevent any collapsing and allowing the right hand to close the clubface. In the short game we often play shots where we try to prevent the right arm rotating over the left until well after impact in order to get sufficient height and accuracy and this is one such instance. This is an important point to understand, and best observed in the top professional golfers. The steep angle of attack in the swing squeezes the ball between the clubface and turf, imparting a lot of backspin,

which sends the ball high into the air, preventing it from rolling too far on landing. But do not expect the ball to back up on the green unless you hit it very hard and also have a receptive green. Golf played on well watered courses, such as those in Spain and America, will allow such spectacular shots to happen, but anyone playing on the firm British courses in the summer must still expect the ball to roll on landing. Obviously if you are pitching to a green that slopes steeply towards you, the ball will stop quickly, as will a shot played to a green well below you or into a strong wind. Also those players who use the softer covered balata ball will be able to impart more spin than those using the surlyn. Many professionals will deliberately leave themselves a full pitch into a green rather than play a very short shot. This way they can hit the ball harder, and get maximum spin and control. The par-5 15th hole at Augusta is one such instance where if they cannot reach the green in two, they lay up well short of the water, then hit in a full shot.

Judging distance

When playing any shot in the short game, it is important not to strive too much for distance. It must be remembered that the short game is one of accuracy and not length. It is no use thrashing a wedge 100 yards if it misses the green — better to have hit a 9-iron and swung within yourself. Short irons hit hard do not always go further but do tend to go higher as there is more backspin, so it really does not make sense to try to go for length. The first thing you must find

Mastering the long pitch

out is how far you can reasonably expect to hit your short irons, say, 8-iron to sand wedge. Using the above set-up and swinging in a controlled manner, rather than flat out, hit about 10 shots with each of your short irons, preferably in calm conditions and on even ground. Pace to the centre of each group and make a note of the distance. Therefore, if you find out that you hit your wedge 90 yards, under normal conditions, you should not be trying to hit it 100 yards out on the course. Instead, use a 9-iron.

It is also relevant to find out how far you actually carry the ball with each iron as so often you will be hitting a shot in over a bunker or other hazard, and knowing how far the ball carries, as opposed to pitches and rolls, would be helpful. Either have a friend assist with this exercise, or practise on a soft patch of ground where the ball will pitch and stop. Obviously, you can vary the length and pace of the swing to alter the distance of the shot, but also experiment by going down the grip of the club.

The low flying pitch
If you are pitching into the wind, you will not want to loft the ball too high into the air where the wind will affect it. Instead, you want a shot that will go a little lower, hold its line and not run too far on landing. Those golfers who play mostly on exposed links courses will have to use this type of shot. The main adjustment comes in the set-up, where the ball is positioned nearer the right foot than for an ordinary pitch. This change will mean that effective loft is taken off the club, and so, depending on how far

In the backswing, the wrists will be fully cocked by the time the arms are just past waist height. After impact, do not allow the right hand and arm to rotate over the left, as this will cause the clubface to close too soon

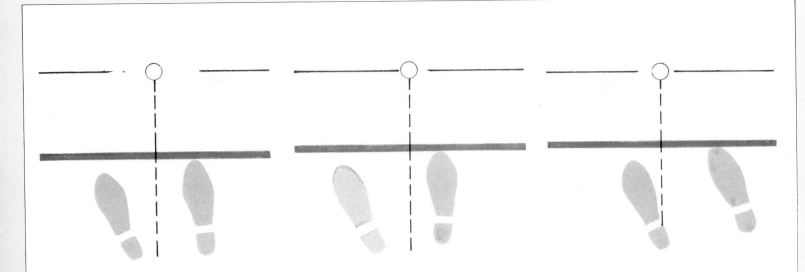

NORMAL PITCH
The feet are close together, open, and angled slightly towards the target, with the ball about 3 inches inside the left heel. The ball is struck while the clubhead is travelling towards the target

LONG PITCH
The feet are open with the right foot at right angles to the line of flight. Since the ball is positioned nearer the right foot, it is struck earlier in the swing, and therefore often hit to the right, unless the clubface is closed or the aim adjusted

HIGH PITCH
The feet are well open, and angled towards the target. Since the ball is positioned opposite the left instep, it is struck later in the swing, and may be pulled left unless the clubface is set open

back the ball is placed, a wedge will be more like a 9- or 8-iron. Address the ball with the hands gripping down the club and well forwards. With the weight favouring the left leg, you are in a position to hit well down on the shot in a firm-wristed manner. As with the basic pitch, the follow-through is short. In playing the ball so far back, and with the weight well forwards, there is a tendency for the ball to go right of where you are aiming, so allow for this by aiming either slightly left of your target, or close the face a little at address.

The high pitch
You may be faced with playing a shot over a tree onto the green, where maximum height is necessary. The best club to use for this is probably your sand wedge as it has most loft. But you must remember also that although this club can send the ball very high, it will not send it very far, so always assess these shots carefully. It would be useful to spend some time finding out how high you can hit your

wedge and sand wedge. You can open the clubface and increase the loft quite considerably, but as you gain height you lose length. Some manufacturers are now making a pitching club that has approximately 60 degrees loft (five degrees more than the average sand iron) and this will hit the ball very high.

If you do have a tree to go over, you must first hope for a decent lie – from bare ground you would be better advised to play under it. But, from a good lie, open the face on your wedge or sand wedge and position the ball opposite your left instep. Your feet, hips and shoulders must aim left of the target, enabling you to swing steeply across the ball to target line from out-to-in. Your weight should be marginally favouring your right foot, and your right shoulder and side will feel much lower than the left. Since your hands are set about level with the clubhead, the shaft being near vertical, the wrists become very active early into the backswing, which is made largely by your hands and arms.

The clubhead is then swung under the ball, but although the hands on this shot are working hard, again the clubface must not close on impact since you require maximum loft for the shot. Therefore, to help keep the clubface square, the legs must move through the shot as well. This particular pitch is played with an action much like a bunker shot, and since all effort is spent on sending the ball high, it will not roll much on landing. Different combinations of clubface angle, hand action, and angle of attack will produce a variety of shots, which can be learned only by experience.

Summary
From these three different types of pitch, you can play an assortment of shots, which will improve your ability to score well. It is only by practising them and learning how the ball reacts to different combinations of club selection, set-up and swing path, that you will gain the confidence to use them and lower your scores.

Playing out of bunkers

Most high handicap and many other club golfers dread going in a bunker, knowing that their ability to get the ball out is sadly lacking. There is no mystery attached to playing out of bunkers, although getting the ball very close to the hole every time will certainly take more than 30 minutes' practice a year. There is even a specially designed club to help with this shot – the sand wedge. This club has a flange which sits lower than the leading edge and, when used correctly, helps the club to skim through the sand, rather than cut too deep a swathe. If you are using a pitching wedge for your bunker shots, you are making life more difficult for yourself. There are certain times when you would use a wedge – for instance, from hard sand – but most of the time the sand iron is the right club.

The set-up and swing
You must first set the clubface open to the target, i.e. pointing to the right. This brings the flange more into play and also puts more effective loft on the club. But when you turn the club open, you must do it by aiming the clubface first and then taking your grip. It is no use just turning the clubface and your hands as well to a new position – your hands must be in their normal place with the clubface spun open. Most grips these days have a ridge down the back and you will now feel this is a different, although perhaps somewhat uncomfortable, position. Do not, however, allow this to cause you to revert to your old grip – practise it and it will soon start to feel acceptable.

To offset the fact that the club is aimed right, and to encourage a steeper swing, you should aim yourself left of the target. So if the clubface is aimed 25-30 degrees right, you aim yourself the same amount left. The ball is played from a point opposite the left heel and there should be more weight on the left leg. You must wriggle your feet into the sand, which gives you not only a firm base, but a chance to find out the texture of the sand – a perfectly legitimate move. As you have dug your feet into the sand, your hands are nearer the ball, so grip further down the club to compensate. Your eyes must focus on a spot in the sand about one-and-a-half to two inches behind the ball, which is where the clubhead will enter. At this point

Gary Player, probably the world's finest bunker player

you must make sure that the clubhead does not touch the sand as this would incur a penalty. Hold the club just above the sand, at the point where you want the club to enter rather than right behind the ball. The hands and arms swing the club up quite steeply in the backswing with the body turning very little. Do not fall into the trap of just picking the clubhead up with your hands as this only provides a stabbing action. Concentrate on swinging your arms up in the backswing and letting your wrists cock naturally. There is little weight transference to the right, and therefore a minimum of leg action. But, during the downswing, they must work in unison with the arms, so that the weight moves well onto the left side and the clubhead can be kept open through the shot. The left arm must keep swinging to a high finish and must never be overpowered by the right side. So all you have done to play a bunker shot is to aim the clubface right, your body left and swing along the body line, i.e. out-to-in from the target, entering the club into the sand about two inches behind the ball.

The pace and length of the swing are important, and all thoughts of rushing into the bunker and taking a quick stab at the shot must be dismissed. The club should be swung almost leisurely and, for the beginner, a full backswing and follow-through are a must. The more proficient golfer can start to vary the length and pace of his swing, safe in the knowledge that the mechanics are correct. If you have trouble just getting the ball out of the bunker, first work on a swing that is full, enters the sand about two inches behind the ball and is not too fast.

The most common faults
Most faults tend to start at address and bunker shots are no exception. Golfers with bunker problems usually address the ball with the clubface too square to the target, so that the

An explosion of sand and ball marks this bunker shot by Fuzzy Zoeller

Playing out of bunkers

round soled flange of the club is not really effective. In turn, they normally have the ball too near the centre of the stance, and the body too square on. From this set-up, they usually play a sharp-wristed jab, burying the clubhead in the sand, with the ball driven forwards too low and more often than not landing back in the bunker.

For a shot from a bunker where the lie is reasonable, i.e. the ball is not buried, you are trying to play the ball out high so that it lands softly with little roll. Therefore, by opening the clubface, and setting yourself in a position to cut across the shot, you should achieve the desired effect. By swinging the club through the sand and keeping the left arm moving into a high finish, the ball will sail out. Many golfers try to scoop the ball out and they fall back on the right foot and hit the sand much too far behind the ball. You must remember on bunker shots that you are trying to hit down and through, removing the area of sand on which the ball is sitting, which will in turn remove the ball.

A good practice routine for bunkers is to draw a line in the sand where you want the clubhead to enter and then, without the ball, just swing the club, trying to enter the sand on that line. By not having the ball there, you can concentrate solely on hitting the sand in the right place and taking a fairly long shallow divot.

Keep the address position relaxed with the shaft coming straight up towards you. The hands should not be ahead of the ball which should be opposite a spot just inside the left heel

Whereas professionals and more experienced players may appear to use a wristy action, they have tremendous hand and eye co-ordination, and have no doubt practised regularly. In contrast, the average club golfer needs a reliable swing action – one that will not require too much timing. Your main aim is to swing your arms up without too much body action and then feel as though you are almost dragging the clubhead through the sand into a high finish.

Plugged shots

When a ball is plugged, the bottom is lower than normal, so you cannot hope to hit a shot where the club cuts under the ball. Instead, you have to concentrate more on hitting down on the shot in order to get deep enough into the sand. To start, dig your feet further into the sand than usual, which will help the club to penetrate deeper. The ball must be positioned more towards the centre of the stance with the weight on the left side. We have already established that by opening the clubface, the flange comes into effect and helps to prevent the clubhead digging into the sand too deeply. Therefore, since you are now trying to penetrate the clubhead further into the sand, you must keep

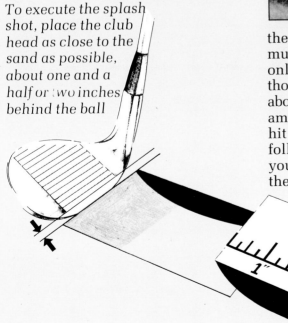

To execute the splash shot, place the club head as close to the sand as possible, about one and a half or two inches behind the ball

Nick Faldo hits through the sand

the clubface square, not open. You must also take a squarer stance, with only the feet slightly open. All swing thoughts now are on hitting down about an inch behind the ball, but the amount of sand you will be trying to hit through will prevent much of a follow-through. Think of swinging your arms straight up from the ball on the backswing, then driving down and through as far as you can go. The ball will come out lower than normal and run on landing.

Hard sand

This is the time when you should consider using a wedge instead of a sand iron, since it has no flange. Set-up as you would for a standard bunker shot, but remember that the club has less loft so the ball will go further. Alternatively, if you position the ball towards the centre of your stance, you can use your sand iron, since from this position, the flange will not bounce so much. Swing a little steeper and hit closer to the ball.

Judging bunker length

Today's professionals display a superb ability for judging the distance of bunker shots. They naturally spend a great deal of time practising this skill and building up a register in their minds of how the ball reacts in different circumstances. The club golfer, once he has acquired a decent technique for getting out of bunkers, can then start on the same procedure as the top class player – of discovering the range of shots he can hit. Distance gained from a bunker can be affected by several factors, i.e. speed of swing, amount of sand taken, loft of clubface and the type of sand in the bunker.

Method 1

Once the beginner has learnt how to

From this position, top professionals such as Jack Nicklaus would expect to get the ball very close to the hole

set-up correctly, he should practise trying to send the ball the same distance each time, with the same strength swing. Therefore, the clubhead must enter the sand at approximately the same spot in relation to the ball each time, and this in itself has to be the first skill to acquire. Like all other shots in golf, control of the clubhead is vital. Once you can reliably reproduce this shot, it is time to experiment by opening the clubface

further, so that it now faces even more to the right of the target. Aiming your body an equal amount to the left and swinging at the same speed, you can produce a higher, softer shot which does not go so far. The club is swung in line with your shoulders – out-to-in to the target line – and it is the resultant increased slicing action and loft on the club that produce a softer shot from the same swing. By using the same strength swing all the time and varying the amount the clubface and body are open to the target, the height and distance of the shot are altered. You can see also how the ball reacts when you reduce the angles from your original set-up, and, from opposite ends of these examples, you will discover the range of bunker shots you can hit with the same swing. It will take a while to get used to seeing the clubface look so open on some of these shots, but the results will be encouraging.

Method 2

From the original set-up for bunkers, the clubhead should enter the sand about two inches behind the ball, but by altering this entry point, you can vary the distance of the shot. The further behind the ball you hit, the more sand you take, and therefore the blow to the ball is cushioned even more and it does not go so far.

Obviously, the nearer to the ball the clubhead enters the sand, the less sand is taken and the ball goes further. Again, practice will benefit this method, and you need to realize how much resistance there is when the clubhead enters the sand four inches behind the ball. There could be the

Judging bunker length

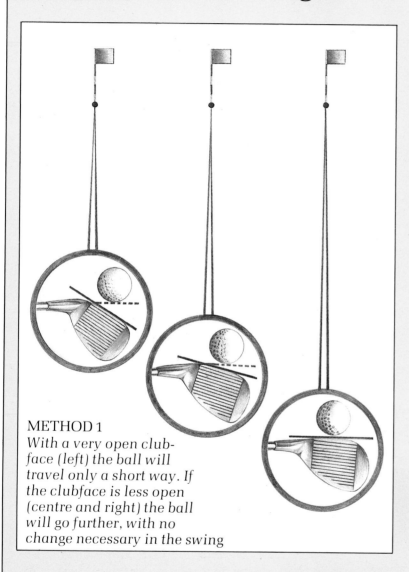

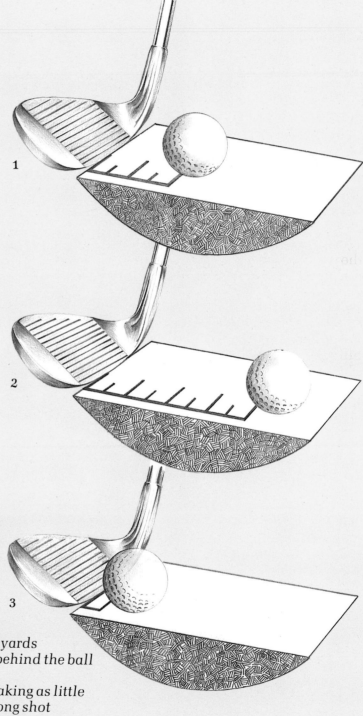

METHOD 1
With a very open club-face (left) the ball will travel only a short way. If the clubface is less open (centre and right) the ball will go further, with no change necessary in the swing

METHOD 2
By varying the amount of sand taken, you will affect the distance the ball will go
1 Hit about 2 inches behind the ball
for a shot of about 8-10 yards
2 Hit about 3-4 inches behind the ball for a short shot
3 Hit the ball cleanly, taking as little sand as possible for a long shot

tendency to quit on the shot, and so you must make certain you still swing the clubhead through the sand. The danger when trying to strike the sand, say, one inch behind the ball, is that you could take the ball too cleanly and send it too far. So accuracy is important in this instance.

Method 3

The third way of varying distance is to alter the strength of the swing, leaving the clubface and body line in the same position, and the point of entry the same. The benefit of this method is that you only have one variable, i.e. strength of swing, whereas the set-up and point of entry remain constant. The bunker shot therefore tends to resemble much more a shot from the fairway, in that you concentrate only on the pace or length of the swing for distance. This is the method used by the more advanced player, since there can be problems for the high handicapper when it comes to hitting shorter bunker shots with this method. In this instance, the backswing would not be very long and there is the possibility of either slowing down completely and losing all momentum in the swing, or of using the hands too independently at the last minute to achieve some pace.

Naturally there are limitations with this method, but when they are reached, the more advanced player will be capable of incorporating any part of the previous two methods into his game. In fact, top professionals spend a lot of their practice sessions working on the different combinations possible and noting the results. They would also experiment with different sand wedges since they do not all produce the same results.

The long bunker shot

Perhaps the most difficult shot to judge from a bunker is one between approximately 40-80 yards. Here you have to consider the angle of the bunker face as well as the distance. From a steep bunker it may not be possible to gain enough loft to clear the face and gain adequate distance to reach the target, and so a compromise of getting out as far as possible is essential. If the face of the bunker is shallow, distance can be attained by striking the ball first, instead of the sand. You may choose to use a sand wedge, wedge or 9-iron to produce a variety of shots, but the swing should not be rushed. To make sure that the ball is hit before the sand, some people find it useful to look at the top rather than the back of the ball.

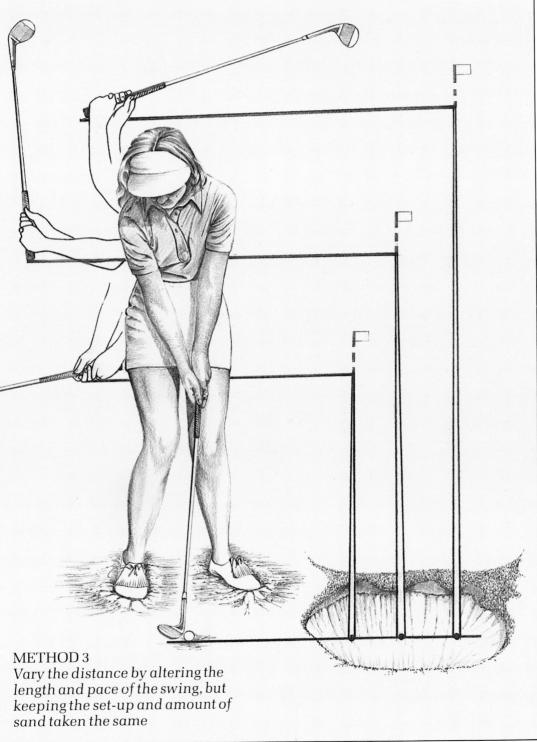

METHOD 3
Vary the distance by altering the length and pace of the swing, but keeping the set-up and amount of sand taken the same

Downhill bunker shots

Play the ball well back in the stance. The weight should be on the left foot so that the body is at right angles to the slope and with the shoulders following the lie of the slope. The vertical body position on the right is incorrect. This will often cause the player to hit too far behind the ball

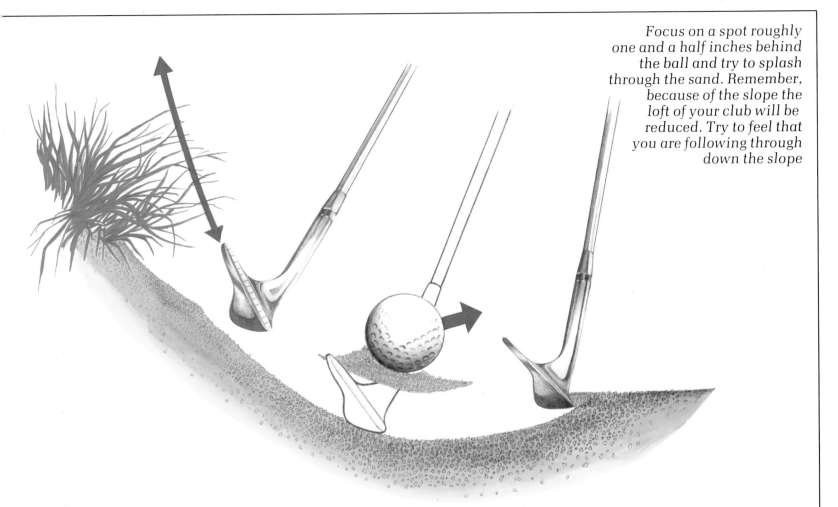

Focus on a spot roughly one and a half inches behind the ball and try to splash through the sand. Remember, because of the slope the loft of your club will be reduced. Try to feel that you are following through down the slope

The downhill bunker shot can be quite justifiably described as one of the most difficult in golf and must therefore be treated with respect. From a steep downhill lie, with the green high above the ball, it might prove more beneficial to even play out sideways or backwards, such can be the degree of difficulty involved. But like all shots in golf, if the situation is approached sensibly with some knowledge of how to play the shot and how the ball will react, then there is every chance of playing an acceptable recovery.

Address position

Since the area of sand behind the ball is higher than from a flat lie, you have to make sure that the clubhead does not hit the sand too far behind the ball. The best way to ensure this is to set-up with more weight on the left leg, and the right will be more flexed than normal. This, in turn, sets the shoulders almost parallel to the line of the sand and will enable you to produce a very steep backswing. The body is set almost square, rather than too open to the target. The ball should be positioned back in the stance towards the right foot, and consequently the hands will be ahead of the ball. It is important to feel as balanced as possible before you make the swing, and so one or two practice backswings in the address position will tell you if your stance is firm enough. Be careful when making these little practice swings that the clubhead does not touch the sand at all, or you will incur a penalty. The clubface should be only slightly opened, so that the flange does not come into play too much and cause the clubhead to skim over, rather than penetrate, the sand. The 'ball back' position subtracts effective loft from the club, and then the temptation is to open the blade, but since this brings the flange into play, it defeats the original object.

The swing

The set-up puts you in a good position to make a steep backswing, which is particularly necessary if you wish, first of all, to avoid hitting the sand on the backswing and incurring a penalty; and, secondly, to get the clubhead travelling down and under the ball. The swing is made by the hands and arms, with the wrists almost breaking as the first movement, while the weight remains on the left foot. As the downswing begins, the wrists must maintain the angle set at the top of the swing, since if they release too early, the clubhead will contact the sand too far behind the ball. By changing direction slowly, and easing the knees towards the target as the hands and arms swing down, the correct contact about one-and-a-half to two inches behind the

Downhill bunker shots

ball should be made. Then the clubhead must swing down along the contour of the sand for as long as possible, finishing fairly low to the ground. The high handicap player tends to want to scoop the ball up and out of the bunker, but that results in disaster. The main thought must be to swing the clubhead up and down the contour of the sand throughout the whole shot. On severe slopes, you may even find that you have to bend the left arm on the backswing in order to get the club up quickly enough to avoid the sand.

How the ball reacts

The ball on these shots will always come out lower than normal and run further on landing, so make the necessary allowances for this. Do not expect to hit a high floating shot, when even the top professionals are prepared to accept that there are limitations. If the green is high above the bunker, you will need to consider whether playing out in the direction of the pin presents too great a risk of not getting out at all.

At all costs you want to get out of the bunker in one shot, even if you are not on the green. So, if the situation calls for it, survey the surrounding area and work out where you would most like to take your next shot from. Most golfers would rather be playing from the fringe of the green or even the fairway rather than the bunker, so by being realistic, you can get out of the bunker and then have the chance to chip and putt.

Summary

To successfully play downhill bunker shots, align your shoulders parallel to the sand with more weight on the left leg, and the ball more towards the right foot than for normal shots. With the clubface fairly square, make a steep backswing, cocking the wrists early and maintaining the wrist cock well into the downswing. The clubhead must be swung down the contour of the sand, finishing low to the ground. Do not rush the change of direction of the swing, and do not be too ambitious.

Even professionals have nightmares about this sort of lie and, as Bernhard Langer shows, concentrate on maintaining their balance

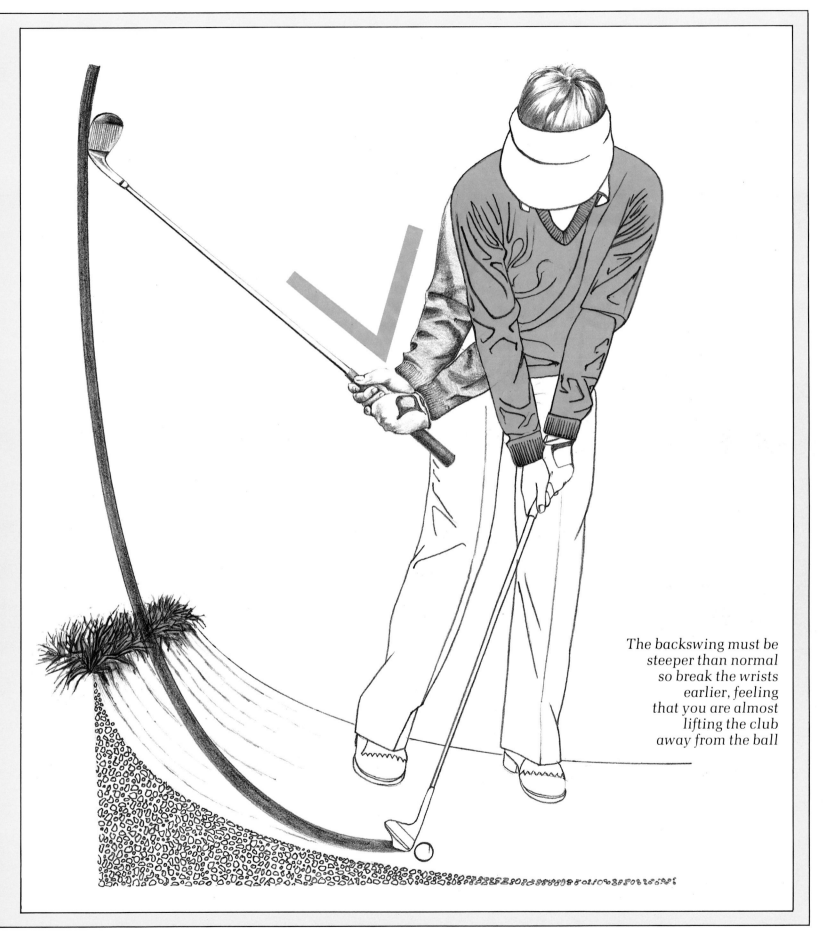

The backswing must be
steeper than normal
so break the wrists
earlier, feeling
that you are almost
lifting the club
away from the ball

How to hole more putts

The first thing to get right is the grip. The putting grip is slightly different to that used in full golf shots. The normal grip for full shots has to control the clubface but it also has to create an abundance of clubhead speed. The thumbs, therefore, are somewhat over the shaft so as to create the necessary freedom of wrist action.

But in putting you do not need distance as such. You do require the control of distance, and so the grip you use has to be slightly different. The putting grip illustrated here is the one most commonly used by good players and is commonly referred to as the reverse overlap.

As is clearly shown, the last three fingers on the left hand and the first three fingers on the right hand hold the shaft, while the first finger of the left hand overlaps the first three fingers of the right hand.

This grip is not absolutely necessary for good putting but it is important that the palms of the hands are opposite, with the thumbs more or less down the shaft. With the full golf shots the clubface tends to open in the backswing and close in the throughswing; with the palms opposite each other, the clubface can more easily be kept square to the swingpath throughout the stroke.

The stroke
Turning to the stroke itself, it is important to make contact with the

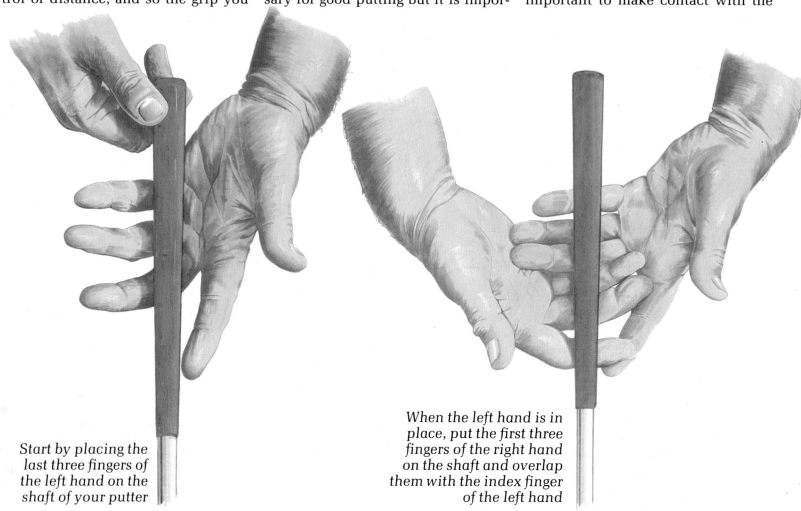

Start by placing the last three fingers of the left hand on the shaft of your putter

When the left hand is in place, put the first three fingers of the right hand on the shaft and overlap them with the index finger of the left hand

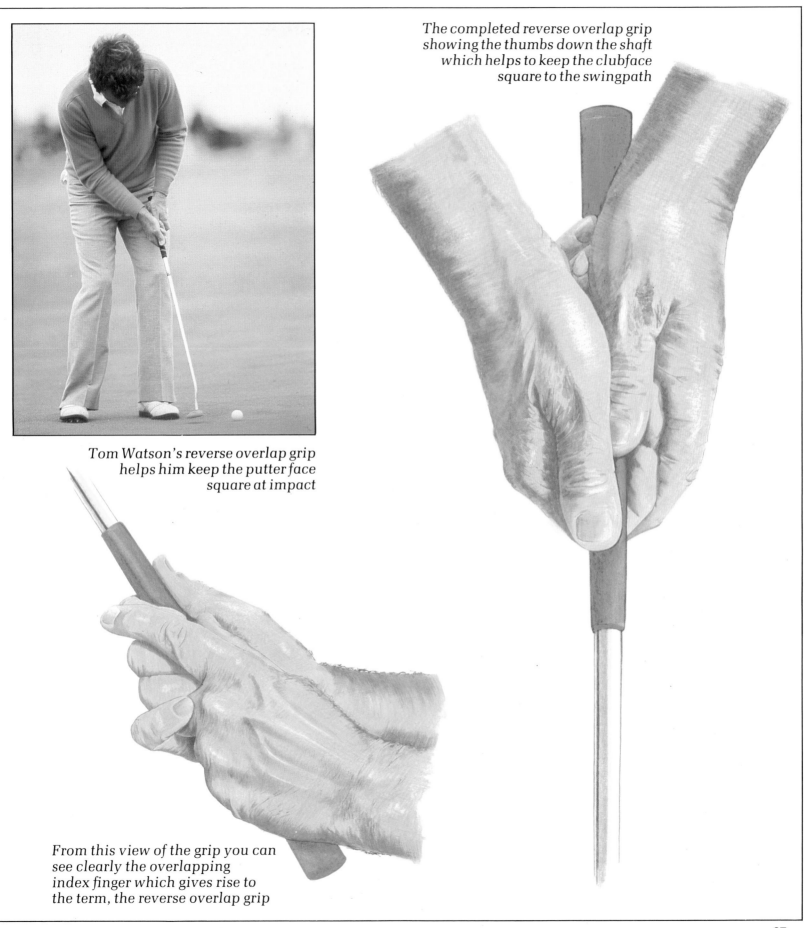

The completed reverse overlap grip showing the thumbs down the shaft which helps to keep the clubface square to the swingpath

Tom Watson's reverse overlap grip helps him keep the putter face square at impact

From this view of the grip you can see clearly the overlapping index finger which gives rise to the term, the reverse overlap grip

How to hole more putts

clubhead travelling on line and with the clubface square to that line. The fact that the ball is to the side of you necessitates that the clubhead approach the ball from the inside in order for it to be travelling on line, with the face square, at impact.

From inside to straight-through maximizes distance with the long shots – it is the feel of distance for putting. Distance is even more important than direction since a putt other than one that is absolutely straight requires the ball to be rolled at a specific speed in order for it to take the contours in the right proportion.

If you do not consider yourself a good putter you should address the ball in the orthodox manner with the clubface pointing down the line, and the feet, knees, hips and shoulders all parallel to that same line. Whether you swing the putter predominantly with the wrists or arms or shoulders is very much a matter of preference but whichever method you choose must be made easily repetitive. For most of us this usually means a combination of wrist and arm action.

The ball is obviously not very far away from the feet at address and therefore the putter head does not swing in very much but it should be of paramount importance on anything other than the shortest of putts. It would only be true that the putter went straight back from the ball if the lie of the club was such that the shaft would be absolutely perpendicular to the ground.

Many players try to take the putter head straight back from the ball which inevitably forces a hit to the left. Before long these players auto-matically react with a quick opening of the clubface at impact. This action is often referred to as the 'yips'. It comes about through a misconception of the desired arc which will then *release* the putter head along the desired line.

The correct length of swing should be one that creates the necessary putter head acceleration through the ball; too long a swing will obviously decelerate at impact whereas a too short backswing has the effect of a sudden acceleration devoid of feel and often resulting in excess body movement which in itself throws the putter head off line. If you are suffering on the greens, practise using a swing distinctly longer or shorter than you have been doing. This often leads to a realization that the swing has not been of the desired length.

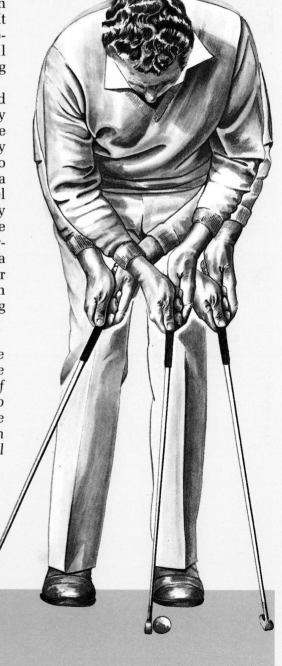

This illustration shows the ball not far away from the feet. The correct length of swing varies from player to player but it must create putter head acceleration through the ball

1

2

3

4

5

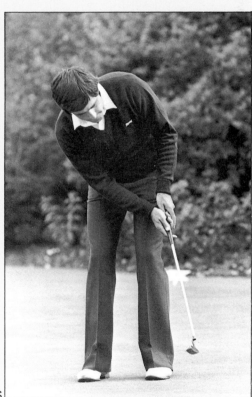

6

The legendary putting stroke of Severiano Ballesteros combines sound fundamentals with tremendous touch. At address(1) he is relaxed and concentrating on the line he wishes the ball to take. Starting the backswing(2) with a smooth takeaway there is no sign of wrist break as he completes the backswing(3). Approaching the ball(4) with the left wrist leading and the blade square to the line. Just after impact(5) and the head has remained still and only starts to come up(6) well after the ball is on its way

Two keys to better putting

When talking about putting there are two distinct elements involved. One is reading the green in order to be able to set the ball off at the right pace and in the right direction, and the other is the development of a sound stroke to facilitate correct striking of the ball.

The great putters have the gift of being able to read the line and see the way into the hole. This ability to read greens can be a tremendous asset, of course. We have all had days when we are able to see the line and it is on these occasions that all of us putt well. We become very positive with our stroke. Conversely, when we are not sure what the ball is going to do this doubt has its effect on our striking of the ball. Jack Nicklaus is a great reader of greens and his penchant for fast greens reflects his confidence in being able to read the line, which, of course, is so much more important when greens are particularly fast. Nicklaus is also known not to be fond of slow greens; his very address position, with the ball particularly forward in the stance, gives the impression that he finds it easy to set putts off in the right direction coupled with his wonderful feel for pace.

In terms of how we lesser mortals should approach this problem of the line, we can only look from behind the ball to the hole and from the hole back to the ball and form a judgment as to how the green is going to affect the roll of the putt. Some days you can do this and be quite confident that you are correct in your judgment. It is on these occasions when you are not sure, that it is *vital to commit yourself to a line* and make sure you set the ball off along it with complete authority. This is of vital importance on the short putts, i.e. those from two to eight feet. To be still hesitant about the line when you are striking the ball is fatal. Most of us when we are practising short putts are quite good, since after the first two putts we know the

Gary Player demonstrates his great putting skill

line and therefore everything is much easier. *Commit yourself to a line before you strike the ball.*

In terms of the stroke, it should be one that makes contact with the club travelling along the desired line with the clubface square to it. Dealing with the clubface first, it is important that your palms are opposite each other with the back of the left hand square to the line. This helps to keep the clubface square to the swingpath throughout the stroke. With the longer shots, the left hand is turned over the shaft to some extent, which allows the clubface to open in the backswing and close in the through-swing. This is necessary since, with the longer shots, we are not only looking for direction but also much more power. To achieve an impact with the clubhead travelling along the line it is necessary on all but the shortest of putts for the clubhead to approach the ball on an arc slightly from the inside.

The forward press

Those of you who are familiar with the putting methods of many of the American circuit players, who as a group must surely be the best in the world, will have recognized that many of them have a forward press immediately before taking the putter back from the ball. Many would stress that this is to give them a firm left wrist at impact which helps to keep the clubface square through the ball. However, this forward press has the added advantage of directing the putter head back on the desired slightly inside arc.

In practice terms, a club shaft

When putting you may choose to adopt the reverse overlap grip. The index finger of the left hand overlaps the fingers of the right

should be laid along the ground and the ball should be positioned close enough to it so that a measurable distance of, say, one inch is left between the toe of the putter and the shaft of the club on the ground. It will be found that if the putter head is taken back the correct amount on the inside (and it is relatively little) when the ball has been struck, the putter head will finish with the toe of the club the same one inch from the shaft. When this is achieved you know the club-head is swinging through the ball in the correct direction. On long putts the putter head will, of course, return slightly to the inside and will finish its arc further from the shaft on the ground than the original position.

Winter evenings spent practising indoors, with the hands warm are far better than when the hands are cold during outdoor practice at that time of the year.

Practise medium and long-distance putts since if this element is good there will not be such a strain on short putts. All the good putters are marvellous at rolling the long ones absolute-

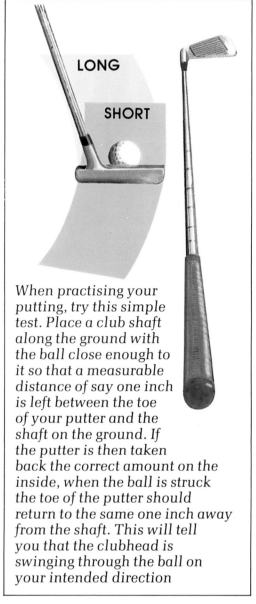

When practising your putting, try this simple test. Place a club shaft along the ground with the ball close enough to it so that a measurable distance of say one inch is left between the toe of your putter and the shaft on the ground. If the putter is then taken back the correct amount on the inside, when the ball is struck the toe of the putter should return to the same one inch away from the shaft. This will tell you that the clubhead is swinging through the ball on your intended direction

ly dead. Distance is more important than direction since other than on a perfectly flat green there is no line to the hole unless you can hit the ball at a particular pace.

Summing up then, practise lots of long putts and if the strike is from inside to straight through, this releasing of the putter head along the line is a great help in feeling the distance. Develop this inside to straight through stroke by practising with a shaft on the ground or, if indoors, by hitting putts parallel to the skirting board in a warm room. And on short putts never strike the ball without first committing yourself to the line.

Three tips to better putting

With all shots in golf, it is pointless getting the strength right if the direction is wrong. In putting, your eyes are more over the ball than at any other time and therefore lining-up should be easier. However, because you are at the side of the ball, visual distortion is still a problem. There are three ways of improving your aim. With long shots, it is advisable to have an intermediate target about three feet ahead of the ball, and in putting you should use a similar routine. Standing behind the ball, pick out a mark about two feet ahead on your line to the hole, then aim to putt the ball over that mark.

Your eye line could be another reason for bad putting. Ideally the eyes should be virtually over the ball, or just inside. To check where they are in relation to the ball, take your putting position and then drop a ball from under your eyes to the ground. If you are in the right position, the ball should hit the putting ball, or drop just inside it.

You may also experience lining up problems if your eyes are not angled correctly. To check this, maintain your putting set-up, take your putter in both hands and hold it parallel to the ground, across the bridge of your nose and immediately under both eyes. Then, without moving the club, raise your head about a foot and you will see in which direction the shaft is pointing. If it is anywhere other than straight to the hole, reposition the angle of your eyes accordingly.

Plumb-bobbing is a method used to determine which way a putt will break

When putting, your eyes should be over or just inside the ball. To test if your eyes are in the correct position: from your putting stance, drop a ball from beneath your eyes and, if you are correctly set-up, it should strike the putting ball or fall just inside it

To check the angle of your eye line: assume your putting position and, with the putter in both hands and parallel to the ground, place the club under your eyes and cross the bridge of your nose. If your eyes are at the correct angle, the club should point to the target

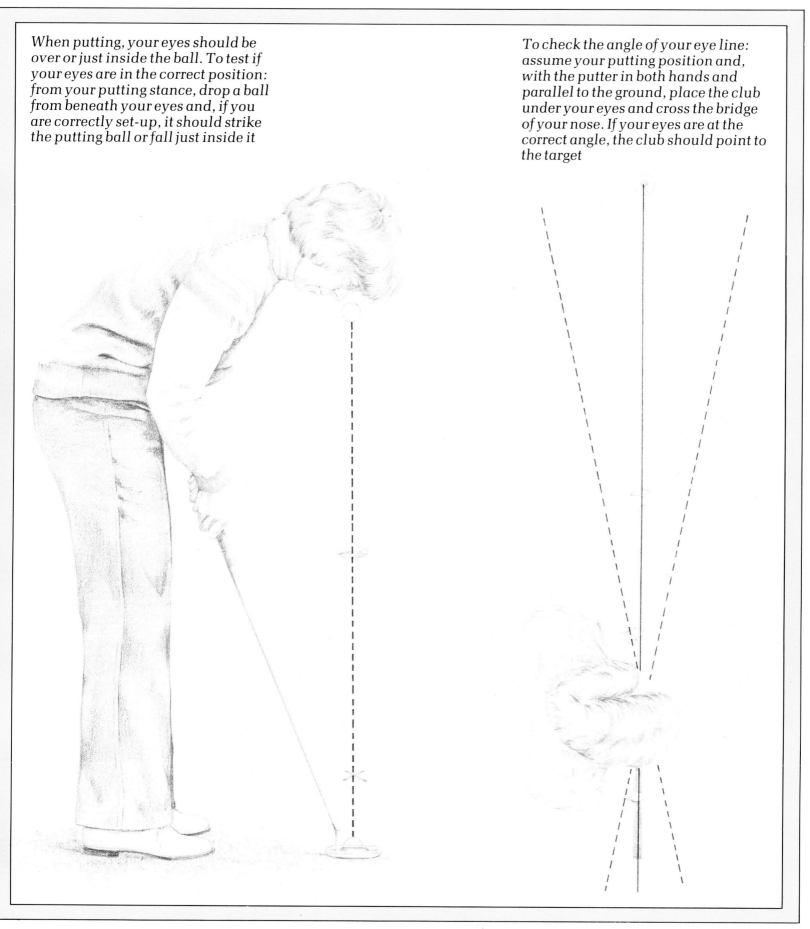

Every golfer, at sometime or other, is afflicted by a particular kind of bad shot. Knowing what causes these bad shots can help you to eradicate them. This chapter analyses the cause and effect of bad shots and provides you with the steps to cure them. Here, you can discover why the slice and the pull are closely related, why golfers who push the ball are also liable to hook it, how to stop topping plus a cure for that most dreaded of golfing ailments – the shank. Learn how to avoid an overswing and dismiss the myth of the late hit. Whatever bad shot ails you, this chapter provides an easy-to-assimilate cure which will soon have you hitting the ball correctly and with renewed confidence.

The slice

The most common swing fault among golfers is undoubtedly the one that produces a left-to-right flight on the golf ball – in other words, a slice. You must understand at the outset that any shots that curve to the right are struck with the clubface open. This invariably leads to an aim off to the left, conscious or otherwise, allowing for the shot. This aiming off to the left leads also to an out-to-in steep, open-faced impact resulting in shots lacking in power which start left and curve to the right. The direct control of the clubface is dependent on the way in which you hold the club. In the simplest of terms, you are endeavouring to hold it at address in a position you will be in at impact.

Golfers with a tendency to slice need to have the 'V's between the thumb and first finger of both hands pointing towards the right shoulder. Although the grip is the direct control of the clubface, it is not the only control. There are many golfers with very strong hookers' grips who still manage to slice consistently. The swing path itself also has a tremendous bearing on the clubface. Once again, you should remember that you are playing a game with the ball positioned to the side of you. It follows then that the arc of swing will be from the inside to straight through at impact and inside again on the follow-through. This type of arc through the ball will allow the clubface to close in sympathy with the arc. A left-to-right flight of the ball indicates that the clubface is open and the swing path itself is out-to-in.

At address, slicers invariably position the ball too far forwards in the stance, which means that the ball will be struck on the follow-through side of the arc when the clubhead is travelling well left of the target. This arc will automatically block any closing of the clubface, since over-riding all attempts to swing the club correctly will be an involuntary blocking of the hands in a vain attempt to propel the ball in the desired direction. This blocking action will, in effect, leave the clubface open even if the grip itself is correct.

At address the ball needs to be positioned far enough back in the stance, towards the right foot, to allow the shoulders to be square or even closed. The hands should be slightly forward of the clubhead, *which will appear to be fractionally open*. This address position makes it possible to swing the club into the ball from the inside,

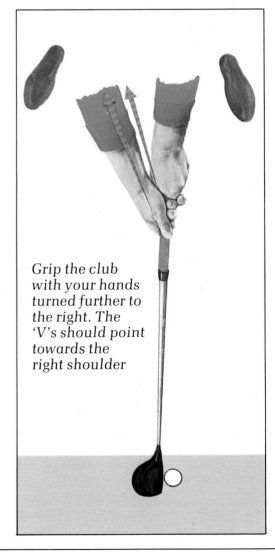

Grip the club with your hands turned further to the right. The 'V's should point towards the right shoulder

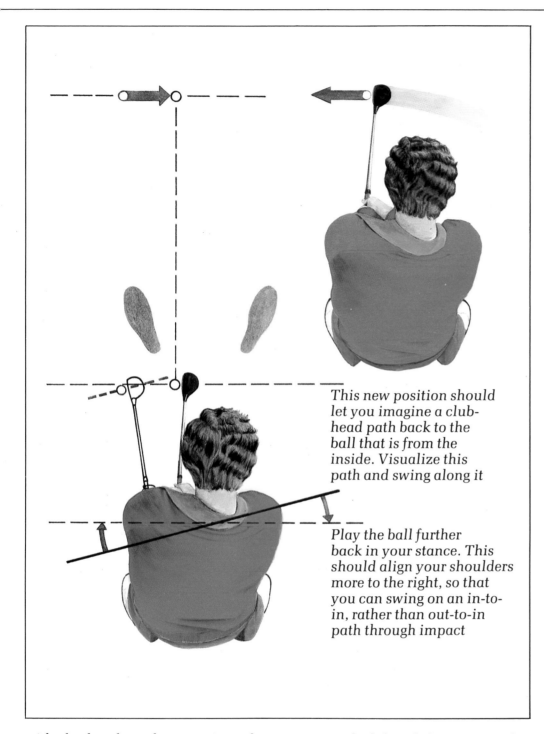

Although the clubface is square at address, the slicer will return it to the ball in an open position with the arc of the swing blocking any closing of the clubface

This new position should let you imagine a clubhead path back to the ball that is from the inside. Visualize this path and swing along it

Play the ball further back in your stance. This should align your shoulders more to the right, so that you can swing on an in-to-in, rather than out-to-in path through impact

If rolling the clubface open is your problem (white arrow), then keep the clubface looking at the ball for a while during the first part of the backswing on an inside path

with the hands and arms, since the swing path can be visualized before the club is moved.

The reaction of this approach of the club to the ball will be one of clearing the hips out of the way, thus allowing the clubhead to move from the inside to straight through to the target. The clubface, open in the downswing, will square up at impact.

To sum up, if your long shots tend to start to the left and slice away to the right, then position the ball further back in your stance and close your shoulder position. Make sure that your grip is one with both 'V's pointing to the right shoulder. Swing the club down from the top with the hands and arms from the inside, clearing the hips in unison with the downward swing of the club. Swing from the inside and clear the left side.

The hook

The hook is often referred to as the good golfer's bad shot and while there may be some truth in that, it is also possibly the most destructive of bad shots in terms of landing the ball in deep trouble. In curing a hook it is important to be reminded of the inter-relationship between the clubface, swing path and angle of approach of the club to the ball. Of these three impact factors, the clubface is by far the most important since if this is in-correct it will affect the other two adversely, too.

All shots that hook bend in the air to the left and are struck with the clubface closed at impact. This type of flight, creating fear of going to the left in the player's mind, invariably leads to an in-to-out swing path. This swing path leads to an upward hit through the ball. In other words, the bottom of the arc arrives too early, that is, behind the ball. This type of action is usually fairly successful when the ball is teed up, particularly if there is enough loft on the club to obviate the closed clubface. However, with the bottom of the arc behind the ball, any shot from off the ground becomes very difficult, particularly when the ball is lying 'tight'. The flight of the ball, which is a direct reflection of the clubface position at impact, has a real bearing on the swing arc that we all use. Much swing instruction ignores this vital fact. The perfect swing arc does not hit good shots unless the clubface is also cor-rect at the moment of impact. This is why so many players claim good practice swings, since with no ball the clubface element of the swing is totally ignored. There are two ways in which the clubface is affected: direct-ly by the grip; and, secondly, by the

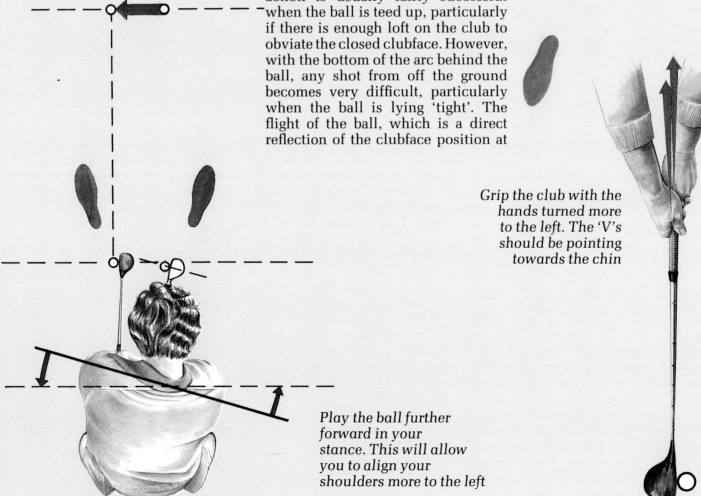

Grip the club with the hands turned more to the left. The 'V's should be pointing towards the chin

Play the ball further forward in your stance. This will allow you to align your shoulders more to the left

swing path itself. Golf is made more difficult because when things go wrong our natural reaction is apt to make things worse.

When shots begin to bend to the left, often because of a faulty grip, we react by swinging the club into the ball too much from the inside. This, in itself, creates extensive wrist roll which tends to close the clubface even more. A hook, then, is hit with the clubface closed with the swing path approaching too much inside, with the bottom of the arc behind the ball. Therefore, our first endeavour must be to get the clubface square.

Those players with the ability to accelerate the clubhead usually need to grip the club in what is described as a 'weak' position; that is, with both 'V's between the thumb and first finger of each hand pointing to the chin. If you hook the ball, this is the first step to getting the clubface square. You should also make the pressure on the grip the same in both hands. If the left hand is tighter than the right, the right wrist will become too active in the hitting area relative to the arms, thus closing the clubface.

When shots are bent consistently from right to left, then it is probable that the set-up is closed and the aim is to the right of the target. The ball then should be positioned further forward in the stance, towards the left foot, and the right foot and shoulder advanced to create a feeling of being more open. It must be remembered that the grip is not in isolation of the other set-up factors and that this more open set-up will encourage a weaker grip. From this address position, it is important in the downswing to combine a feeling of swinging the club down at the same time that the left side is cleared. Initially, to anyone who has been hooking shots, the swing path will feel out-to-in and, therefore, the bottom of the arc much further forwards than hitherto. The basic function of the backswing is to get the club shaft in a correct position relative to the target. It is important to consciously swing the club up on to the target in the backswing as opposed to just pivoting and allowing the club to follow the shoulder turn too closely resulting in a flat arc of swing which also tends to close the clubface at impact.

To sum up, at address weaken the grip, position the ball more forward in the stance and feel the shoulders and feet are more open. From this position, concentrate, in the backswing, on swinging the club up on to the target and, as the club is swung down, clear the left side.

How to avoid skying

Skying is not one of the most common faults but it is something that almost every player experiences at some time or another. It is extremely annoying to watch the ball soar skywards, possibly travelling twice as high as forwards, particularly as the shot is usually straight.

A skied ball is clearly the opposite of a topped shot, and as a topped shot occurs when the clubface is above the ball at impact, so a skied shot occurs when contact has been made with too much clubface below the centre of the ball. There is a simple reason for this and, in essence, it is because the clubhead is picked up sharply at the start of the swing outside the intended line of flight and is then chopped across on the downswing from outside-to-in. Through snatching the clubhead up and away there is little or no pivot. The action gives a steep backswing, and chop down into the ball must follow. Trying to hit the ball further than is humanly possible is one of the causes of a steep pick-up so it is important to remember that the club must be swung smoothly and the clubhead kept low to the ground at the start of the swing.

Skying can occur also if the player keeps too much weight on the left foot during the backswing. This will cause the left shoulder to dip, and a steep, narrow backswing will result. To prevent this, make sure your weight is distributed evenly at address and start the backswing by keeping the clubhead low to the turf for the first twelve inches.

Remember that in order to get the ball travelling forwards, the clubhead must approach the ball parallel to the ground several inches before the ball is struck, and it is the loft of the clubface that will propel the ball upwards. Many players feel that they have to help the ball upwards with a 'scooping' action and throw the clubhead at the ball from the top of the swing. This action makes the clubhead pass the hands before impact and thus it produces contact below the centre of the ball.

When using a driver, it does not always follow that teeing the ball high produces a skied shot. The average player does not sky the ball from a high tee but the chronic skier will sky

A skied shot happens when the downswing is too steep, especially when using the driver. This usually occurs when the club has been picked up on an outside path during the backswing (dark shaded area). A low sweep on a slight curve at the start of the backswing will cure this (light shading), presenting the clubface to the ball moving along and through from in-to-out, giving the correct loft for the club being used

Throwing the clubhead from the top contributes to skying and is usually brought about by slogging or scooping. At impact the weight is forced back on to the right side, the right shoulder drops and the right hand 'flaps' under with the result that extra loft is added to the clubface and power is reduced

a shot from either a low or a high tee. In fact, players with a steep angle of attack into the ball will invariably tee the ball low as they feel that, with a high tee, the club will pass right underneath the ball. Players who do this should tee the ball higher and try and sweep it away with the clubhead travelling nearer the ground on the backswing and throughswing and on an in-to-out path. Skying is a close companion of the slice and is caused by a narrow, steep swing arc. If you widen and flatten that arc then the problem will be eradicated.

How to cure the push

The push is often regarded as the good golfer's error as it occurs when the club is swung on an exaggerated in-to-out track with the clubface square to that line. In producing the push, the golfer has achieved many of the correct movements required for good striking but has probably moved the body ahead of the ball before it is struck.

There are two main causes of this: firstly, a sway to the left on the downswing which is due to the player not releasing the clubhead through the hitting area; and, secondly, addressing the ball too far back towards the right foot.

When a player sways to the left, generally starting halfway on the downswing, both his body and hands are positioned ahead of the ball at impact. The clubface has no chance of squaring up to the intended line of flight. Should the swing be on an in-to-out track the ball will fly straight to the right. With this type of pushed shot, the clubface will eventually reach the square position a few inches after the ball has been struck.

A sway to the left can be caused also by swaying to the right on the backswing. The sway to the left is by way of compensation and the player usually overdoes it. Once again, this puts the hands and body ahead of the ball at impact.

Curing a sway

To stop a sway on the backswing make sure the clubhead starts round on an inclined plane. This makes the body rotate and thus it will not move out of the space it occupies at the time of address. In addition, make sure that you start to release the clubhead during the first part of the downswing so that it will be freewheeling past you. At impact it will have reached maximum speed and will have become almost an independent body. Sometimes a player may have a good backswing and still sway into the ball. This generally happens when the hands have tightened up, usually through anxiety. The clubhead cannot be released and the player takes the clubhead through the shot with a body sway to the left. But if the swing is in-to-out, a push to the right results and sometimes the ball is half-topped.

Wrong ball position

A pushed shot can result also without any sway should the ball be positioned too far to the right of centre in the stance. Then the clubface will meet the ball before it has time to square up correctly at the bottom of the swing arc, which, during a proper swing, is always left of centre.

It follows, therefore, that by having the ball positioned to the right of centre at address the body and hands will naturally be ahead of the ball at impact. The effect is exactly the same as playing the ball from the accepted position and swaying to the left on the downswing. In each case the clubface presents itself to the ball – with an in-to-out swing – square to the direction the club is following but open to the intended target line. Another cause of pushing is through a flat inside backswing. The player swinging on a flat plane rolls the clubface open (clockwise), which means it will be wide

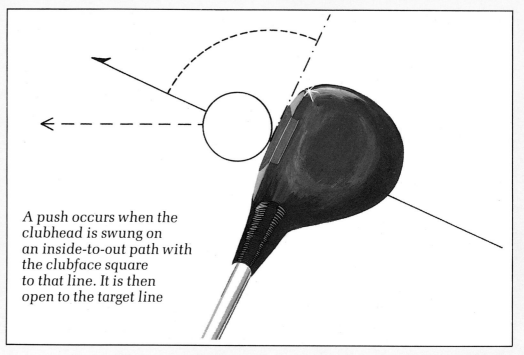

A push occurs when the clubhead is swung on an inside-to-out path with the clubface square to that line. It is then open to the target line

If a player sways to the left on the downswing, his body and hands will be in front of the club at impact with the clubface open. The swing's axis moves to the left, causing a half-topped shot to the right, with the bottom of the swing occurring forward of the ball position

To stop swaying to the left on the way back to the ball, release the clubhead sooner or try to get the clubhead to the ball first. This gives maximum speed at impact together with a square clubface

open at the top of the backswing.

When this takes place, the player may not roll it back square to impact. So the face is still open and usually with a flat backswing, returns to the ball from inside-to-out. In trying to square up the clubface, the player rolls the clubhead to extreme proportions and a hook or a smother results.

The remedy for this is to start the swing by making certain the club starts back on an inside path close to the turf, keeping the clubface looking at the ball for a while. This will automatically make the backswing more upright which helps make the swing a little straighter than the shot. Finally, check your grip to make sure that it is not in a weak position – with one or both hands too far round to the left. Should they be in this position even when swinging correctly, you are likely to produce an open clubface through the shot.

Toeing – the causes and the remedies

Toeing is a recurring and fairly common kind of fault which affects all golfers alike. When the ball is struck as little as half-an-inch on the toe side from clubface centre, then the player at impact feels the shaft trying to twist in his hands.

The onlooker may think a perfectly shaped shot has been hit. The player knows otherwise, however, feeling the grip either trying to twist or, if the grip is slack, actually doing so.

Some golfers fail to bring the clubhead back to the ball square at impact and hit the ball from the very tip of the clubface. If they use a wood they could even find a ball mark on the outside edge of the toe.

The main causes for such extreme toeing are allied to sliced and pulled shots. That is, the clubhead has been swung on an out-to-in track throughout the shot. This is often coupled with falling back on the heels, bend-

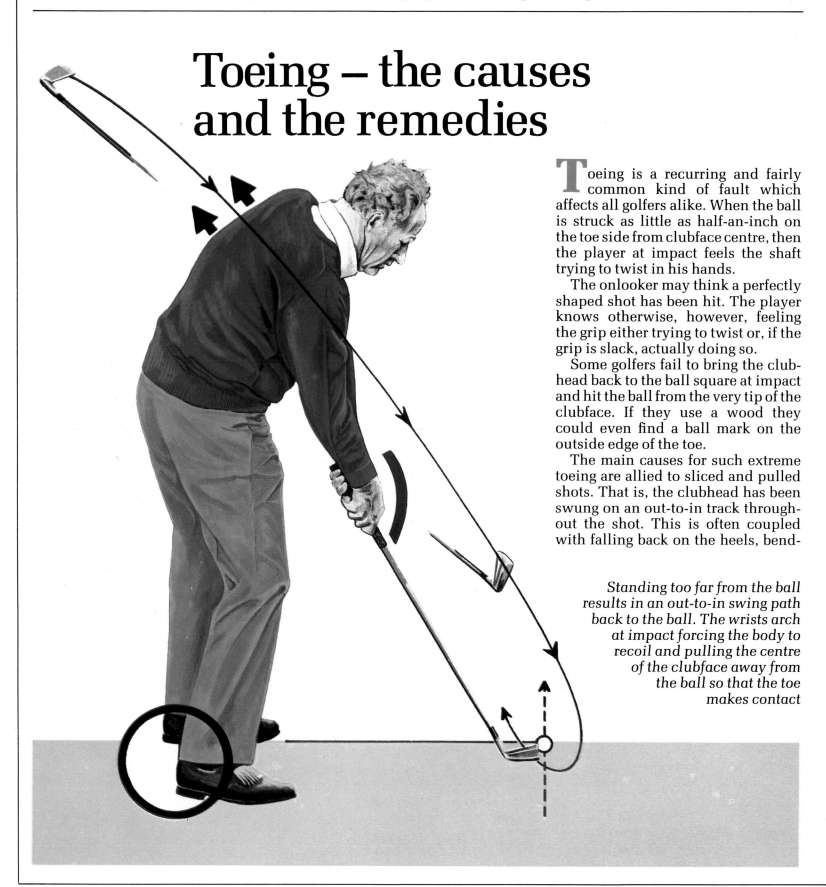

Standing too far from the ball results in an out-to-in swing path back to the ball. The wrists arch at impact forcing the body to recoil and pulling the centre of the clubface away from the ball so that the toe makes contact

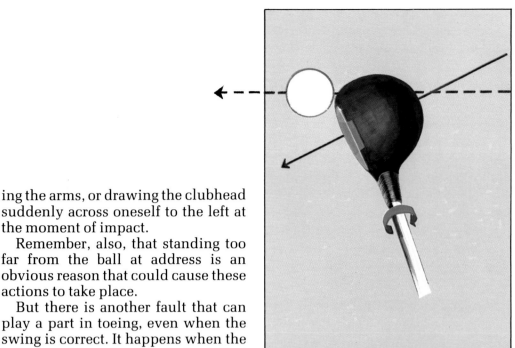

Hitting the ball off the toe is caused by an exaggerated out-to-in swing or by standing too far from the ball, and even a combination of both. When this takes place, the player feels the club trying to twist clockwise in his hands

ing the arms, or drawing the clubhead suddenly across oneself to the left at the moment of impact.

Remember, also, that standing too far from the ball at address is an obvious reason that could cause these actions to take place.

But there is another fault that can play a part in toeing, even when the swing is correct. It happens when the ball is positioned too far to the left at address for the club to be used. The ball will then be struck *after* the bottom of the swing arc has been passed, by which time the club has started its journey around to the finish of the swing.

If you combine the positioning error with any one of the three toeing faults as described, that only serves to magnify the trouble – and you can start looking for those white marks on the toe of your woods.

Most players who toe shots do so as a result of a poor backswing. A similar action causes the pull and slice. The clubhead has been picked up on the outside at the start of the swing, which in turn restricts the left shoulder from turning a full 90 degrees. From this incorrect top of the backswing position, the clubhead will move along a line back to the ball left of the intended line of flight, which is the exact opposite to the circumstances of a shank, when the club is swung too much from in-to-out, combined with a stiff action.

The distance you stand from the ball before playing any shot is of great importance. A large percentage of golfers do tend to stand too far from the ball at address. To them this feels a powerful position. But it will only

make them swing back and through on a flat plane in a scythe-like action. The player has to reach out to make contact with the ball and this brings about loss of power.

Centrifugal force, which is a natural force that recedes from the centre happens with anything that is moving in a circular direction or motion. In golf, at impact, this force is at its maximum and makes the wrist arch and the body stretch.

Centrifugal force can have opposing effects on any shot according to the swing path involved. If the swing is too much in-to-out then the effect of centrifugal force is to make the clubhead move away from the player, and the danger here is that the socket could be sent into the ball. It means, of course, that the clubhead is travelling away from the player.

On the other hand, if the swing should be too much out-to-in, then the reverse can occur. The player recoils backwards and straightens his back a little as the clubhead comes into the ball. It means he will be pulling the centre of the clubface away from the ball and striking the shot off the toe.

So it is easy to recognize by this that it is most important to stand your

correct distance from the ball for the particular club being used, neither too near nor too far. The correct distance will make you swing slightly under yourself and a little on an inclined plane. That is exactly what we are seeking. For how to assess your correct distance, turn to the section on shanking. The over-correction outlined there is designed to help the player to feel the centre of the clubface once again. If this cure is actually overdone it results in the ball being struck off the toe.

So when you think about it, you can see that the cure for toeing is to make the clubhead move on a line inside-to-out. Or, as an over-correction, swing the clubhead out to the right of the intended line of flight. Overdone, of course, the ball could well be struck off the heel. Practice is the answer to achieve that fine adjustment.

In order to reach a correct top of the backswing position, so allowing the player to swing back to the ball from in-to-out, start the backswing round on an inclined plane. This will make the left shoulder turn a full 90 degrees and arrive under the chin by the time the top of the backswing is reached. From such a position, make the clubhead follow exactly the same path by swinging back to the ball and through the whole lot.

But beware. Even if the top of the backswing is correct, it is still possible to hit across the ball by throwing the clubhead out on an outside line in which case, the same cure, just described, will apply.

Assuming that the grip, stance, backswing, and position of the ball at address are correct, then the ball can

Toeing – the causes and the remedies

With the correct swing it is still possible to toe the ball if you position the ball too far to the left. The bottom of the arc has been passed and the clubhead is already moving inside. The dotted line shows the proper ball position

still be struck off the toe through the arms bending just before impact or by falling back a little onto the heels. Keeping the weight on the right foot too long can produce a similar result.

What causes such faulty body movements? As always stated, all body actions or reactions are a direct result of how the clubhead has been swung. One of the main villains of the toeing complaint is our old familiar friend – slogging in an attempt to get extra distance. However, what you need in golf is *swinging power* – not powerful effort – when you are making a stroke.

Another major cause of toeing, when it comes to the high handicapper, is an instinctive fear of not being able to get the ball airborne. Subconsciously the player tries to help the loft on the clubface by scooping at the ball. When this happens, his body reacts naturally by straightening and then falling back on to the right foot with both arms bending.

To overcome scooping, always trust the loft built into the clubface when playing a shot, and imagine you are going to drive the ball low under a tree. The loft on the clubface will give the desired elevation for the club being used, and the body actions, in response, will look after themselves, taking on a new correct form without you trying to make them happen.

As that great teacher of the game, the late Ernest Jones, wrote: "The body and all its parts should be treated as disastrous leaders but as wholly admirable followers of any clubhead swung on the correct path."

Corrections for toeing
1 Check your grip and stance.
2 Check the position of the ball at address, making sure that it is in the correct position for the club being used.
3 Check you are not standing too far away from the ball at address.

To stop a scooping action imagine you are playing the ball under an overhanging tree and drive it along and through. This picture of Jerry Pate is an excellent example of this desired action

4 Check the start of the backswing. The golf swing is more or less a circle and must start with this in mind in order to form one.

5 Check the top of the backswing. The left shoulder should be tucked under the chin.

6 Make the downswing start inside the intended line of flight.

7 Do not slog. Swing the clubhead back to the ball. Swinging creates centrifugal force. This will naturally stop your arms from bending through impact. It also checks falling back on the heels and gives correct weight transference and balance.

8 Resist the temptation to help the ball into the air. Drive it down, forward and through.

The solid figure shows a comfortable address position the correct distance from the ball. The dotted image is standing too far from the ball. Start the swing by making the clubhead stay close to the turf on a slight curve for about ten to fifteen inches. The two clubheads at the top show the respective positions at the top of the backswing

How to avoid topping

Topping is particularly common to beginners but many experienced players occasionally hit the ball straight along the ground at the most inappropriate time. Nothing is more annoying. When you address the ball before swinging you establish a certain distance between yourself and the bottom of the ball. You measure this distance with your left arm and the golf club as you set it on the ground behind the ball. The arm and club combined form the radius of the swing. But during the backswing this radius is shortened considerably because of the cocking of the wrists, and unless in the downswing the wrists are fully uncocked, the original radius will not be re-established. The clubhead just cannot get back to the bottom of the ball.

There has been much stress of leg and body action over the past two decades, and this is understandable since much of this type of advice emanates from the great players. They all swing the club freely with the arms and hands in the downswing and are apt to assume that lesser mortals do likewise. Unfortunately this is not always the case; over-emphasis of body action in the downswing and the clubhead fails to catch up. The wrists are still cocked to some extent when the ball is reached. The beginner's first priority should be to re-establish the swing radius similar to that at address by impact. We

The left arm and club combine forming a radius for the swing

During the backswing you lose a large part of this radius due to the wristcock

If the wrists do not fully uncock, the clubhead does not get back to the bottom of the ball ▶

measure ourselves from the ball at address, and the downswing is a re-measuring of this radius. It also happens to be the striking of the ball with the clubhead – the whole essence of the game.

When shots are frequently topped because the wrists are not fully uncocked there will also be a tendency for the ball to slice since the clubface will be left open. Therefore, follow a practice drill with a relatively easy club such as a 6-iron or a 3-wood with

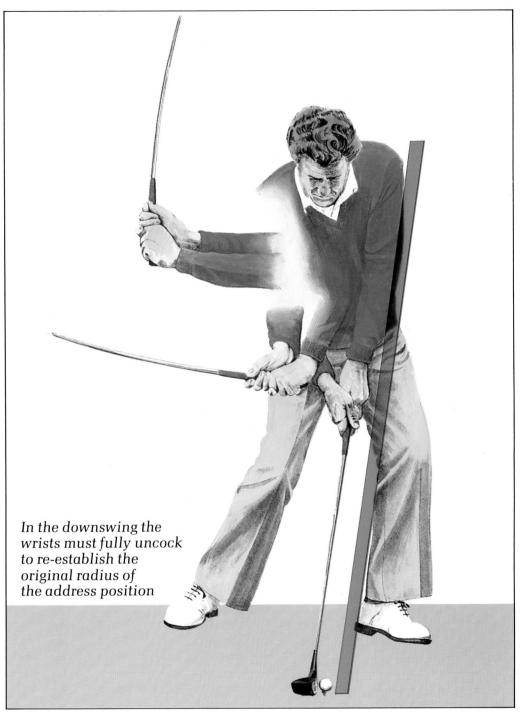

In the downswing the wrists must fully uncock to re-establish the original radius of the address position

the ball teed appropriately, concentrating on reaching the bottom of the arc behind the ball. This sort of thinking retards body action in the downswing and increases the use of the arms and hands so as to arrive at impact with the club shaft and left arm in a relatively straight line at or before impact thus reaching the bottom of the ball with the clubhead.

It should be remembered that the golf swing is a combination of hand and arm action and body action. What is suggested will increase the use of arms and hands and nullify to some extent the application of the body to the ball (usually the shoulders) as opposed to the clubhead. When the ground is being hit consistently behind the ball, obviously you should then begin to focus on the ball itself rather than behind it.

How to stop hitting behind the ball

Hitting the ground behind the ball, or hitting 'fat' as it is popularly known, is a common fault among golfers. To correct this fault, you must remember that the golf swing is a balance of the correct hand and arm action and body action. These elements must be synchronized to obtain the best results. When the ground is being hit behind the ball, the hands and arms will be working from the top independently of the body and, therefore, the radius of the swing (that is the left arm and club shaft) will reach its maximum too early in the downswing. This over-wide downswing will tend to make contact with the ground before you are ready for it.

This action tends to produce hooked shots since the clubhead will have passed the hands and will be closed by the time the ball is reached. To correct this, the player should concentrate on unwinding the lower half of the body at the same time that the arms swing down. Every attempt should be made to keep the legs and hips active so that the hips can be more open to the target before the ball is actually struck.

Many golfers with these particular faults, hitting behind and hooking, have made a conscious effort to grip very lightly with the right hand. The effect of this is for the right wrist to become too active at the top of the backswing leading to a casting action which creates excessive width on the downswing. It is important to grip the club with the same pressure in both hands to avoid separating the hands at the top.

To prevent this separation, practise with a blade of grass placed on top of the left thumb and, with the right palm in place, swing through the ball without dislodging the grass. Even the great professionals like Gary Player have been helped by this suggestion which has improved their game.

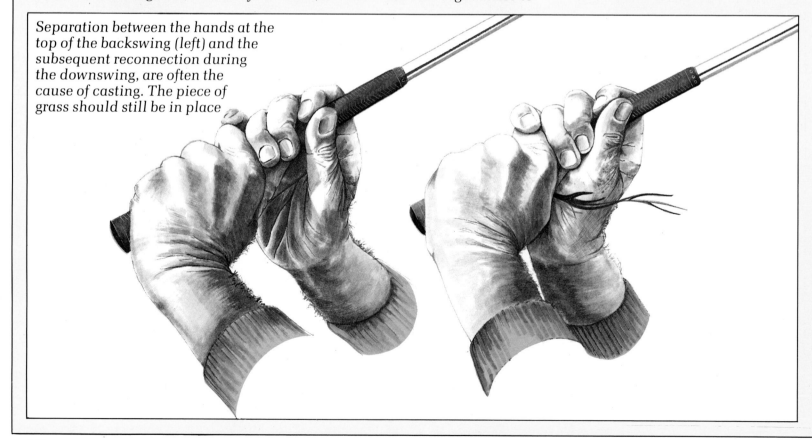

Separation between the hands at the top of the backswing (left) and the subsequent reconnection during the downswing, are often the cause of casting. The piece of grass should still be in place

Make sure you clear your left hip around to the left during your downswing

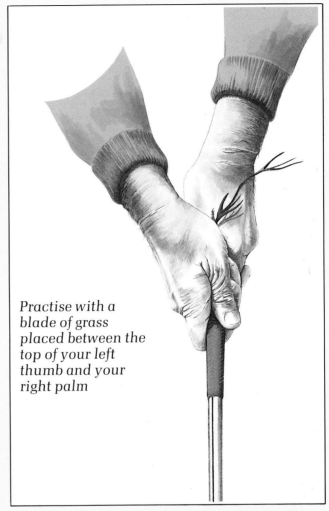

Practise with a blade of grass placed between the top of your left thumb and your right palm

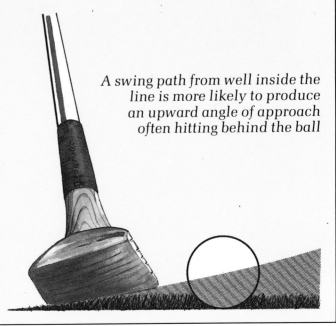

A swing path from well inside the line is more likely to produce an upward angle of approach often hitting behind the ball

Cure your smother and get that ball up

We have all experienced at some time or other, a round of golf when it has seemed almost impossible to get the ball to rise much above ground level. This holds especially true when using the fairway woods and long irons, and you can even find a 7-iron shot flying no higher than a normal 2-iron.

Even with the ball teed up it becomes impossible to attain the hoped-for elevation, and the only time the shot looks right is when driving from an unusually elevated teeing ground.

The more you try to get the ball airborne, the more it hugs the grass. The villain of this particular frustration is the action that produces smothering. The smother is, in fact, related to the hook and has the effect of making the ball stay very low, usually turning to the left.

This kind of poor shot is the direct result of the clubface being hooded at the moment it strikes the ball. The loft built into the club at manufacture has been almost eliminated and it is possible, when using the more powerful clubs, for the loft to be actually reversed. The player has turned the clubface over at impact which makes it impossible, therefore, to hit the ball into the air. In fact, if it was possible, the ball would travel underground.

Now there are various degrees of smothering depending upon how much the clubface is turned over at impact. Should the loft on the club be altered only slightly, then the result is a low-flying ball that will travel, at maximum, only about two-thirds of the normal distance through the air.

We know that it is a hooded face at impact that causes the smother, but what causes the hooded clubface?

There are four main reasons:
1 A poor grip.
2 An incorrect position at the top of the backswing even though the grip may be correct.
3 A lateral sway to the left with the hands in front of the ball.
4 Hooding the face at impact combined with rolling shoulders (producing a smothered pull).

Any one of these four will cause the right hand and arm to overpower the left during the downswing, so turning the clubface over to give a hooded result. To find a remedy, start with the grip, which is the main culprit in smothering. Make sure that the right hand is not round and under the shaft in an over-powerful position. If it is, then it will dominate the left hand and turn the clubface over at impact. Or it could be at address that the left hand is positioned too far over to the right showing three-and-a-half to four

Gary Player holds the clubface square through the shot to avoid a smother

Cocking the wrists too quickly(1) leads to a steep outside backswing, minimal shoulder turn and a piccolo grip with the left wrist under the shaft(2). The downswing starts by throwing the clubhead, as the left hand closes on the shaft(3). To avoid smothering always start the backswing by keeping the clubhead close to the turf(4)

knuckles.

If this is the case, you are in real trouble because this will cause the clubface to close at the top of the backswing. As a result, it will be closed at impact and then a smothered shot will be produced.

You will have to move both hands round to the left until the inverted 'V's formed by the first finger and thumb of each hand appear to you, as you look down (from the bird's eye view), to be pointing up the middle of the shaft. To the onlooker they will appear to be pointing between the player's right shoulder and neck.

At first the alteration in the grip will feel very unnatural, but with diligent practice it will soon become commonplace. With this grip, the hands will not turn the clubface to a closed position at the top of the backswing nor at impact. If, however, the hands have not been altered sufficiently to the position just described, you may get a hook and that is the best you can expect.

A second cause of smothering is a closed clubface at the top of the backswing. This can still be obtained even using a correct grip and is generally caused by rolling the clubface anticlockwise during the swing. Should the player fail to compensate for the faulty movement by not rolling the clubface clockwise on the way back to the ball, it will be hooded at impact.

To check this point, make sure the right wrist, not the left, is under the shaft at the top of the backswing. Do not just swing back and stop to check if your right wrist is in the correct position. It can be done only by an observer, so ask a friend to look for you. Better still, seek the help of your club professional. A half-closed clubface at the top of the swing is what you are seeking ideally.

There is one more fault worth mentioning and that is try not to have a loose left hand at the top of the backswing. When this happens the left wrist is under the shaft. The left hand bends back and opens. This is called a piccolo grip.

When this fault occurs the player

Cure your smother and get that ball up

starts his downswing by shutting the left hand forcibly, which results in a 'throw' of the clubhead and causes hitting from the top. The clubface closes, and if it closes to the point of being hooded, then the result is a smothered shot. So keep the left-hand grip firm during the swing ... but not to the point of being rigid.

Reason number three does not really apply to the driver but does apply with all the other clubs. It is smothering caused by swaying towards the target. Why not so much with the driver? Simply because the ball is teed up and a hooded face in this instance may cause the ball to be struck above the clubface on the paintwork – a weak, high shot will always be the result.

This kind of action is always caused by not releasing the clubhead in the impact area – mainly due to a stiff-wristed action. The player instinctively knows he has to get the clubhead to the ball, but due to his wooden-like action has to sway to the left to make contact. This can also, to some extent, cause the right shoulder to turn too soon. This brings his hands in front of the clubhead at impact with the face hooded and the natural loft diminished.

You can test this for yourself. Stand at an address position and move laterally to the left leaving the clubhead behind the ball. By doing so you will see what is meant. The loft will start to disappear. If this swaying action should be your fault, it is quite easy to rectify by keeping your head behind the ball throughout the backswing and downswing until after impact. This will make you release the club-

Imagine you are swinging round the rim of a wheel with your head serving as the hub. This is the best mental image to have to help cure smothering

An incorrect grip is the main cause of smothering. Too strong a grip, ie, four knuckles of the left hand showing, will cause the clubface to be closed at impact

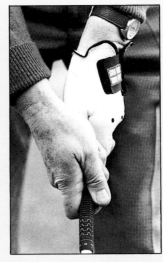

A correct grip should only show one and a half knuckles of the left hand. The back of the left hand should face the target

head through the shot.

Cause number four is the natural one affecting mainly the beginner. It takes place in a swing that is radically wrong from the start, and goes hand-in-hand with a pull-type action.

It happens when a backswing is too steep, so making the downswing outside the line of flight. (This can also cause a slice, but in this instance you are only considering the smother.)

Likewise, it can happen when the backswing is correct but the player, at the start of the downswing, throws the clubhead out and forwards. The right shoulder reacts in response to this movement by rolling round and the clubface becomes hooded with diminished loft at impact.

The cure for the steep backswing is similar to the pull and slice. Assuming that your grip, stance, alignment and posture are correct, make sure that as soon as the backswing commences the clubhead is then made to swing around on an inclined plane, then stay on the path the clubhead started on.

This will give you a correct position at the top of the backswing from which you can deliver the clubhead to the ball on the correct line with every chance of the clubface presenting its true loft at impact.

It is possible that a correct top of the backswing movement can go wrong if the clubhead is thrown out at the very commencement of the downswing.

Should this be your trouble, then make the clubhead swing back to the ball feeling it is going to travel on a path near to your right toe and away from your left as it swings through: in

other words, from inside-to-out. This is an over-correction which will more often than not produce a swing track through the ball going from inside-to-straight.

Finally, it is worth checking on ball position in relation to feet at address. If the ball is too far to the right for the particular club being used, then some of the loft is taken off the clubface.

However, many a good player will want to use this ball position when playing into a very strong wind and hoping to produce a low flying, wind-avoiding shot.

Corrections for smothering:

1 Check your grip, so the inverted 'V's are in their correct place.
2 Have the position of the wrists at the top of the backswing checked. The right wrist, not the left, must be under the shaft.
3 Make sure there is no lateral sway to the left by keeping the head behind the ball until after impact.
4 Check that you start the backswing correctly, and once that is achieved make sure the swing back to the ball is moving on an in-to-out path.

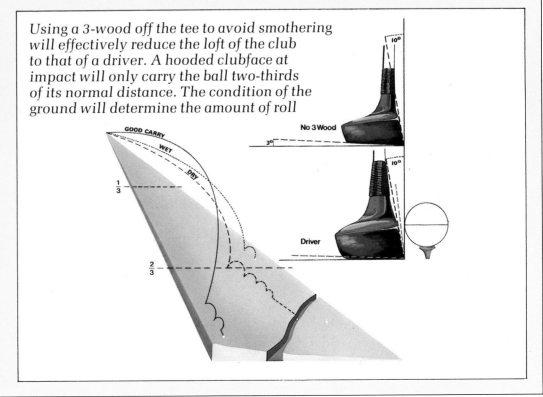

Using a 3-wood off the tee to avoid smothering will effectively reduce the loft of the club to that of a driver. A hooded clubface at impact will only carry the ball two-thirds of its normal distance. The condition of the ground will determine the amount of roll

The myth of the late hit

Advice about late hitting is the enemy of many golfers and the myth of this particular swing position is based on 'frozen' action pictures of the game's great players. Usually, the description accompanying such pictures points out how the player has kept his wrists fully cocked, as an aid to increased power and accuracy, when his hands are waist-high on the downswing. Most golfers who see these pictures assume that this must be an ideal position and set out to reproduce it. However, there is no such thing as late hitting in the first-class player – and assuredly there is no such thing for the handicap player.

What the camera does not show is that the top player's clubhead, at the so-called late hitting position, is catching up the hands all the time so that by the time the ball is reached, both hands and clubhead are together. Any golfer trying to copy the late hitting position has no chance of getting the clubhead to the ball in time. The hands will have gone past the ball before the clubhead can catch up and, at impact, the clubface will be open. The likely result is either a slice or a pull-slice or, if an in-to-out swing path has been maintained, a push or push slice can be expected.

The average golfer should be thinking about the opposite to a late hit and concentrate on getting the clubhead in sooner. Jack Nicklaus himself has said that you cannot get the clubhead to the ball soon enough when seeking power and accuracy. So what is meant by the advice to get the clubhead in sooner? It means that the clubhead must be made to reach the ball just before the shoulders have

returned parallel to the intended line of flight. Do not confuse this with the fault of hitting too early. This occurs when the player throws the clubhead out and around from the top of the backswing, not unlike casting a line when fishing. There is no doubt that 'frozen' action pictures produced by the high-speed camera are responsible for putting more golfers on the wrong path to the late hit than almost any other factor.

The player who copies the late hitting position lacks distance with shots because there is no clubhead speed at impact. When wrist action is deliberately delayed through impact, maximum clubhead speed occurs a long while after the ball has been struck. Many golfers slice as a result and then try to hit even later when seeking a cure. This only aggravates the fault. If you concentrate on hitting late then you will be too late. Let the

The so-called 'late hitting position'. Do not try to copy this position but understand the powers that produce it

natural forces look after themselves and do not try to manufacture them by conscious effort. For a practical test, go to the practice area and hit some shots, deliberately keeping your wrists fully cocked on the downswing. The type of poor shots already mentioned will be produced.

Why then are the wrists seen to be fully cocked at waist height on the downswing? After all, the camera does not lie. It happens because with good players the wrists do not cock to their maximum until they are on their way back to the ball and a subconscious flail-type action is produced. This flail action brings the

By trying to get the clubhead to the ball 'sooner', the clubhead travels at high speed to reach impact simultaneously with the hands

player's hands automatically waist-high on the downswing with the wrists fully cocked. It is this effect, frozen by the camera, that gives the illusion of deliberately hitting late.

In a proper swing this simply happens and does *not* have to be consciously produced. As for the flail, this arises from a change of direction – from the clubhead going back to starting down. Add to this the weight of the clubhead, which during the swing is measured in pounds rather

Getting the clubhead to the ball at the same time as the hands and before the shoulders have turned provides power and accuracy

than ounces, and its speed and you are generating a force of up to a ton at impact. The result of these forces is so great that the wrists will break to their maximum on the way back to the ball in the downswing.

Top players know that they must move the clubhead at lightning speed from the waist-high position so that by the time the hands return back to the ball, the clubhead will have travelled the greater part of its arc and pass the hands at impact. The truth is that this is unlikely to happen and the real effect is for the clubhead to arrive at the ball at the same time as the hands. Therefore, the feeling for which you need to strive is that the clubhead is going to arrive at the ball first. The moral is to forget late hitting (delayed action) and concentrate instead on getting the clubhead back in time along the correct swing path and then you will have the clubface square coupled with maximum speed where it matters most – at impact.

The shoulders and hands have hardly moved but the clubhead is catching up as impact draws nearer

Groove your swing to eradicate the pull

A pulled shot is one that travels in a straight line to the left of the intended target. If you hit a shot that starts out to the left but then curls further left towards the end of flight, then that is a pulled hook. Both these shots occur as a result of an outside-to-in swing path which is why the pull is from the same stable as the slice. However, whereas the slice involves an out-to-in swing path with an open clubface at impact, the pull involves the same swing path but with the clubface square at impact to that swing path line. If the clubface is closed at impact along that swing path then a pulled hook will result.

The first thing to be done when faced with a pull is to stop swinging the clubhead across the line of intended flight. Start by checking the basics: grip, stance, ball position and alignment. When these are in order, the next most important factor is the first movement of the backswing. You should be starting the backswing all in one piece – that is, shoulders, arms, hands and clubhead dominated by the left side around a fixed axis. This makes sure that the clubhead starts back naturally inside the intended line of flight for about the first twelve inches of the swing. Usually from such a start the rest of the backswing will follow to a good position at the top, from where the downswing can be delivered in the correct form.

With an incorrect swing, the one travelling from outside-to-in, the club has been started back on an outside line from where it is impossible to reach the top of the swing in a correct position. If the swing starts outside, then it invariably stays outside and returns to the ball on an out-to-in path. Then the right shoulder moves round in response instead of under, and this, in turn, produces a flat follow-through. Therefore, it is vital to start the swing in one piece as this sets the swing path on the inside.

Although you may start the swing on the inside and reach a correct position at the top, it is still possible to pull the shot by throwing the clubhead outside the line with the initial movement of the downswing. This occurs mainly when the player is striving for extra distance. This action makes the right shoulder turn outwards instead of under the chin.

Assuming that you have reached the correct position at the top, the correct start to the downswing makes the hips and shoulders start to turn towards their position at address. The weight wants to move on to the left foot with the wrists automatically maintaining their hinged position to about waist-level on the downswing.

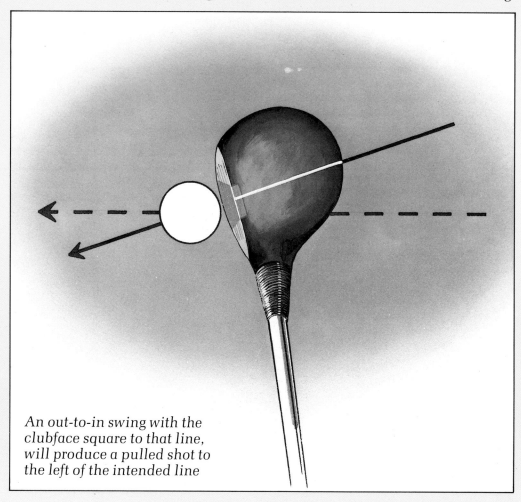

An out-to-in swing with the clubface square to that line, will produce a pulled shot to the left of the intended line

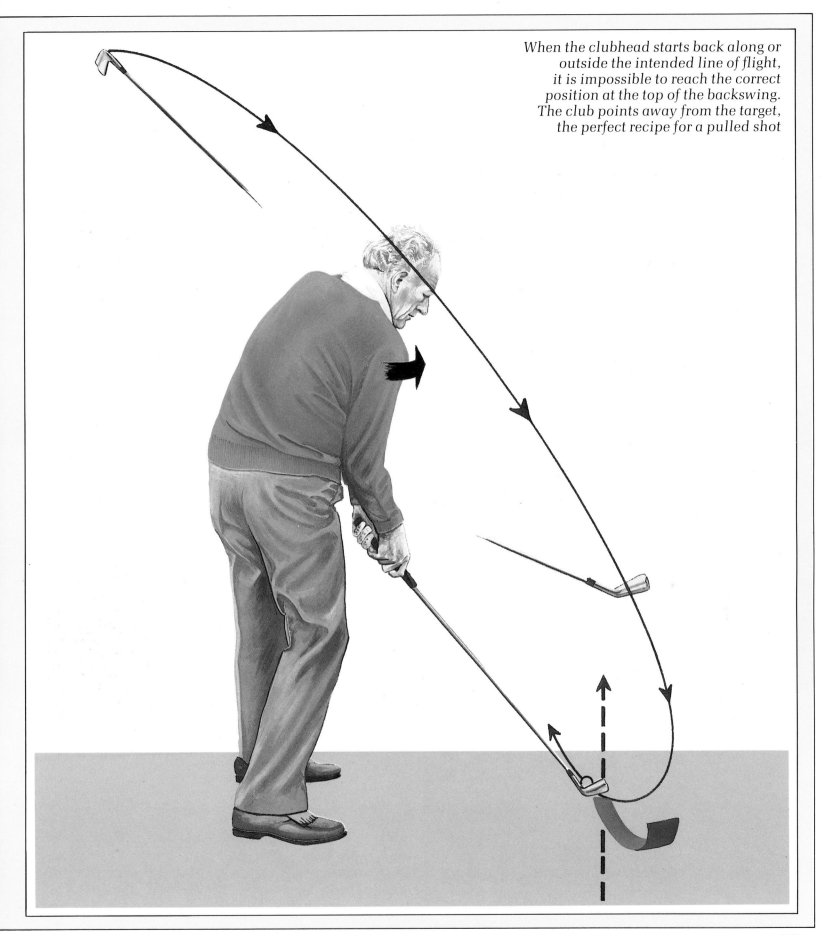

When the clubhead starts back along or outside the intended line of flight, it is impossible to reach the correct position at the top of the backswing. The club points away from the target, the perfect recipe for a pulled shot

Groove your swing to eradicate the pull

As the downswing continues the club gathers speed, and it should have reached maximum speed by the time that impact is achieved, on line, swinging towards the target or even a little to the right of it. The main point is that once you reach the correct position halfway in the downswing then it is impossible to hit the ball from outside-to-in – you have to hit from the inside.

One other point to remember is to position the ball at address inside the left heel. If the ball is too far forward in the stance, either opposite or outside the left toe, then the clubhead will reach the ball as the swing path travels back inside the target line and a pull will result.

However, no matter how long you play, there will be occasions when you succumb to the impulse to apply more power than you can control. Such extra effort will be applied through leverage and forced 'force', which will result in inaccuracy and loss of control. When you are in control of the club during the swing, you can sense what is happening throughout the action of the swing. That makes it possible for the clubface to meet the ball correctly at the moment of impact.

An exaggerated inside takeaway(1) will place the player in an incorrect position at the top of the swing and the downswing will commence with the shoulders throwing the clubhead outside the line and across the ball after impact(2)

Even from a correct top of backswing position, a pull can still occur if the player throws the club outside at the start of the backswing. This usually happens when striving for extra distance

Corrections for pulling

1 Check your outside-in swing. If you pull shots consistently you must be striking the ball from the outside.

2 Check the basics – grip, stance, alignment to target, and ball position – when at address.

3 Check your start to the backswing. The left shoulder, arms, and clubhead must start together.

4 Check the top of the backswing. The clubshaft must be parallel to the target line.

5 Check the start of the downswing. The clubhead must be kept inside the intended line of flight.

6 Check that you are swinging the clubhead and not using 'forced' force.

Avoiding an overswing

In order to hit the ball consistently, you need to control the clubhead throughout the swing. Loss of control on the backswing makes it very difficult for a golfer to reproduce a reliable action. In the cases of overswing, the clubhead bounces around, out of position at the top of the backswing instead of almost coming to rest, as is evident with the world's top players.

Left arm too bent
It is usually the beginner who has not yet fully exercised the golfing muscles in the back who suffers from bending his left arm too much. He looks upon the golf swing as being made purely with the hands and arms, and therefore neglects the part that the body must play in providing a turn in the backswing. By only lifting his arms, in an effort to get the club far enough back, the left elbow has to give and all clubhead control is lost. The remedy here is to feel that the left shoulder moves away at the same time as the arms. At the top of the backswing, the left shoulder should be above the right knee. The shoulder turn will provide width and the correct length to the swing, and take the strain off the left elbow joint.

Loose grip
Grip pressure is one of the more difficult things to define in golf. Many teachers advocate a light grip, whilst others would recommend one that is firmer. However, all would agree that the pressure should never slacken at the top of the swing. At address the pressure in the left hand is applied

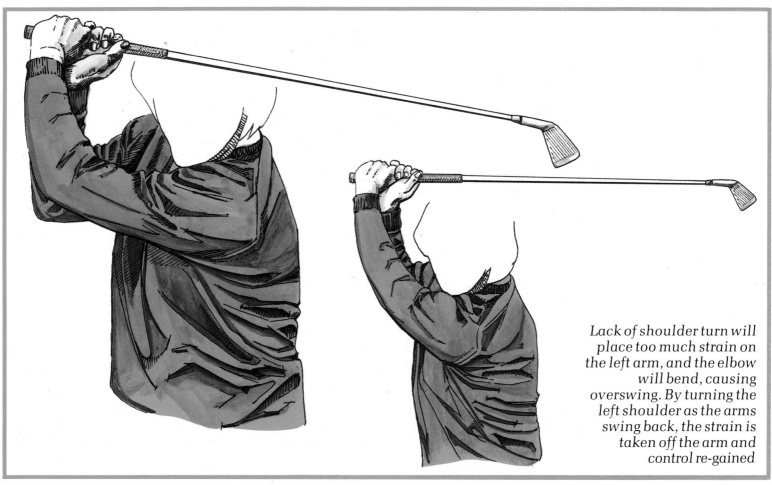

Lack of shoulder turn will place too much strain on the left arm, and the elbow will bend, causing overswing. By turning the left shoulder as the arms swing back, the strain is taken off the arm and control re-gained

1

2

3

4

5

6

7

8

On this wedge shot, Ben Crenshaw retains control despite his long backswing. Starting the backswing(1) and there is an immediate impression of the width of arc he is trying to create as the club continues upwards(2). At the top(3) he has achieved a full shoulder turn but the club is well short of the horizontal and he is poised to thrust off his right side while maintaining the angle between his arms and the shaft(4). Approaching impact and the hands are beginning to release the clubhead(5) and eventually square it up(6). Just after impact and the width of arc created in the backswing is reflected by this position(7), his momentum carrying him on

Avoiding an overswing

with the last three fingers, and in the right, the middle two. At this point the grip should not be sloppy, but firm enough for the player to have control if the clubhead is waggled. As the backswing progresses, more pressure is experienced in the last three fingers of the left hand, and for many the temptation is to release that pressure, and with it clubhead control. Although the grip should not become vice-like at the top of the swing, a player may feel that a slight increase of grip pressure from the address position is necessary to retain control. For most people this is a natural reaction, much like holding an empty glass with a light grip and automatically strengthening it as someone pours in water. But for those whose fingers loosen at the top, a conscious effort must be made to keep the grip firm throughout.

Wrist cock delay
Much is talked and written about in golf regarding the width of the backswing, and the correct way to achieve this is often misinterpreted. Many golfers feel that the clubhead has to be swung back as wide as possible, instead of understanding that width comes as a result of correct arm swing and body turn. Mistakenly, in an effort to keep the clubhead wide for as long as possible, the wrist cock is delayed until the last minute. The sudden pressure on the wrists is more than they can cope with and the hands consequently lose control of the clubhead. As the hands and arms start to swing the club away from the ball, the wrists must start to cock, so that by the time the arms are approaching a position parallel to the

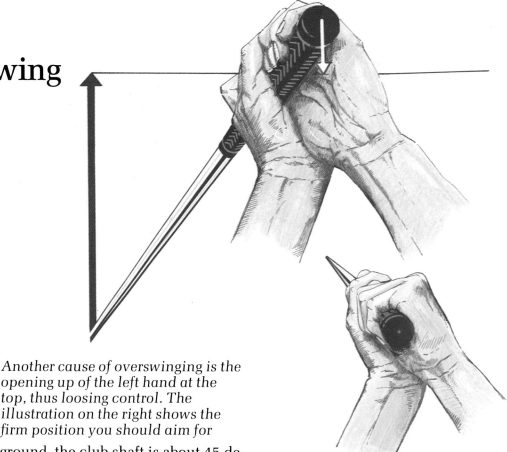

Another cause of overswinging is the opening up of the left hand at the top, thus loosing control. The illustration on the right shows the firm position you should aim for

ground, the club shaft is about 45 degrees to the ground.

A good exercise to develop and feel the correct wrist action is to take your sand wedge and, from a stance about a foot wide, swing your arms back and let your wrists start to break almost immediately. Stop the swing when your arms are parallel to the ground and check where the shaft is pointing. By using the sand wedge, the heavy weight in the head will encourage the correct wrist cock. When you have done this 10 times, take a full swing with the club, and feel the difference in your swing. Transfer this exercise to a middle iron, where you will require a good shoulder turn at the same time as you swing the club back.

Pace and length of the swing
If the club is swung back too quickly, the hands and arms will not be able to

control it. Moreover, when a player swings back too fast he often swings back too far as well, and the best remedy in this case is to slow down the pace of the swing until it is manageable. Many women feel that the faster and longer they make the backswing, the further the ball will go, but a long uncontrolled backswing is useless. One of the best ways to cure overswinging through speed is to practise what feels like a three-quarter swing. This does not mean just lifting your hands and arms to reduce the length and pace, but swinging your arms and turning your body at such a pace that they only make what feels like three-quarters of their usual journey. If many players took one-third off their backswing, and added it to their throughswing, they would be better golfers as a result.

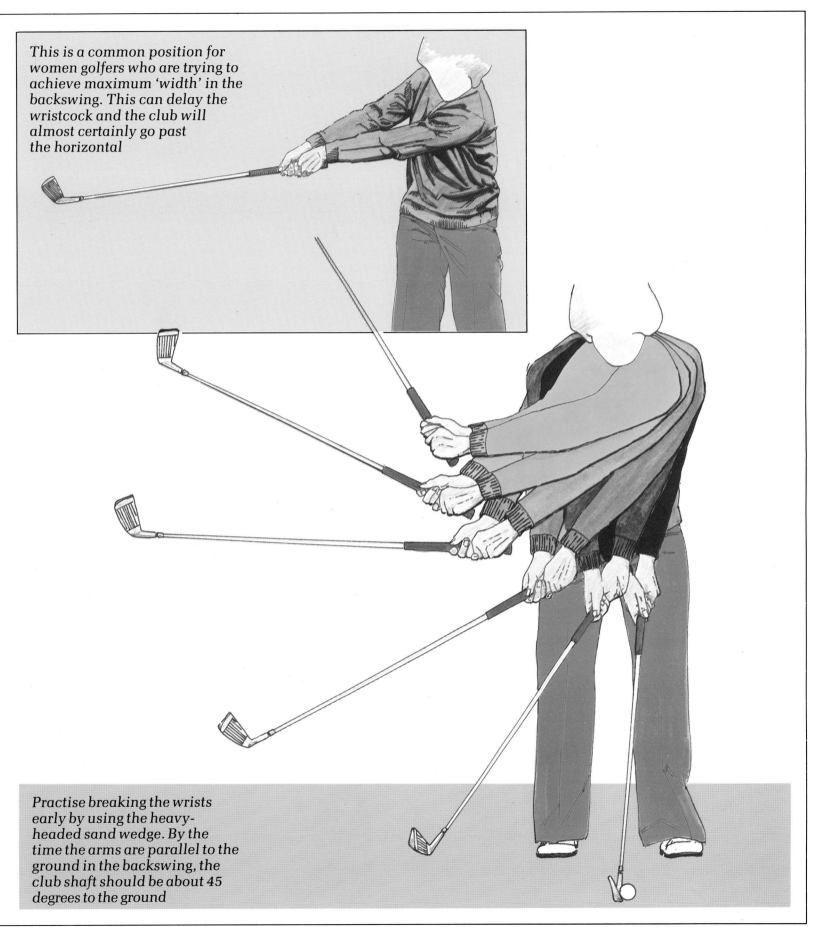

This is a common position for women golfers who are trying to achieve maximum 'width' in the backswing. This can delay the wristcock and the club will almost certainly go past the horizontal

Practise breaking the wrists early by using the heavy-headed sand wedge. By the time the arms are parallel to the ground in the backswing, the club shaft should be about 45 degrees to the ground

Curing the shank

A shank is probably the most destructive and mentally devastating shot in golf for it strikes without warning and invariably sends the ball into an irretrievable spot. There is, however, a very simple cure which, with a little perseverance and use of a practical exercise, should quickly be of help if you have this problem. The position of the ball in golf, on the ground and to the side of you, determines two major factors:

1 The fact that the ball is on the ground means that the club must swing up and down.

2 Because the ball is to the side of you, at the same time that the club swings up and down, it should be on an arc that approaches the ball from the inside, hits straight through and returns to the inside. The backswing should position the club correctly, which takes in two elements: plane and direction. When the club is swung on too flat a plane with the arc too far behind you, it will swing too far away from you on the downswing, thus hitting the ball in the heel of the club with a wooden club and on the shank with an iron. The natural reaction is for the player to stand further away from the ball which in itself creates an even flatter arc and makes things even worse.

Most players with a tendency to shank are not aware that the backswing is made to position the club. They have usually concentrated solely on the pivot on the backswing. If you only pivot and allow the club to associate itself too closely with the pivot, the backswing ends with the club travelling backwards instead of upwards and therefore swings for-wards instead of down in the downswing. The inter-relationship between the clubface and swing arc is such that when the arc becomes too flat, the clubface rolls open far too rapidly during the backswing, and then closes much too quickly on the throughswing.

There are two exercises that can greatly assist anyone with this problem. You are trying to turn the shoulders correctly but at the same time swing the club up so that it finishes the backswing parallel to the

Hitting practice shots with your backside close to a wall will eliminate a flat swing plane

Playing the ball too
far forward at address
aligns the shoulders
too far to the left

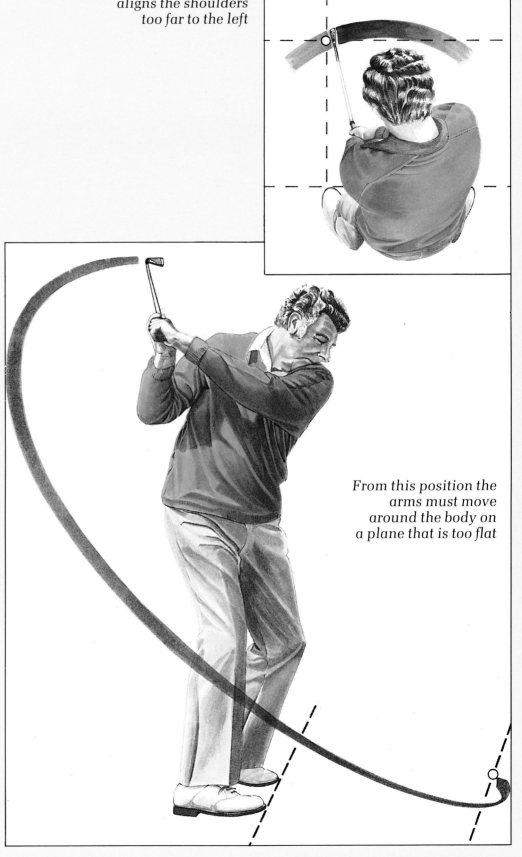

ball-target line. To stop the club swinging too far behind in the back-swing, practice should be done with something in the way of the wrong movement, such as a soft, high hedge. With this obstruction in the way, as the shoulders turn the club is forced on the correct upward arc. Initially the hedge will take something of a beating no doubt but in a fairly short time the desired effect can be achieved and you will improve.

Practising on a slope with the ball below the feet is also helpful. In this situation it is virtually impossible to pivot very much, added to which the downward view of the ball gives you the desired picture of the necessity of swinging the club up and down as opposed to round the body. The feeling needs to be one of swinging the hands, arms and club high enough in the backswing to reach the bottom of the ball, which should be positioned distinctly below the feet.

Both these exercises are most useful for those players who tend to swing the club on too flat an arc, irrespective of whether this actually creates a shank. A flat swing almost always starts from a much too open-shouldered address position. You are trying, remember, to swing the club up on the inside, but an open shoulder situation leads to too much effort being made to get the club inside, hence a flat arc. If you suffer with a flat swing your feeling should be one of having the arc inside by addressing the ball with the shoulders closed, and thus the concentration can be on the hand and arm action. Swing the club up and down on this predetermined inside arc.

From this position the arms must move around the body on a plane that is too flat

Golf is a game where there is always room for improvement. During the course of a round, a golfer is faced with many different types of shot that may require special techniques. Knowing how to handle these various shots can bring immediate improvement to your score. This chapter tells you when and how to shape your shots, how to combat uneven and poor lies, how to get out of trouble and how to utilize your time on the practice ground to the very best effect. As your golf becomes more advanced you will be able to apply these various techniques during the course of an actual game.

When and how to shape your shots

Golf being a game of ball control, it is imperative to accept that what the ball does is totally dependent upon what the clubhead is doing at impact. The clubface can be square, open or closed at impact but it can also be strong (de-lofted) or weak. The swing path can be straight through, out-to-in or in-to-out. Additionally, the club can either be hitting down, up or through (parallel to the ground).

This shows clearly that there are many combinations of the clubface, swing path and angle of approach which will flight the ball in different ways. A particular type of contact may be useful or not depending on the situation. Club selection is also most important since clubs with different lofts will shape the ball differently even with exactly the same conditions at impact.

All things being equal, curving shots in either direction is possible with the straight-faced clubs since the contact is high enough up the back of the ball to apply side-spin. However, it is usually easier to play long shots left to right since right-to-left shots call for a closed clubface, and with straight-faced clubs there is the obvious difficulty of getting the ball in the air. A right-to-left shot also requires a good lie because the necessary in-to-out swing path is particularly shallow.

When trying to play a fade round a right-hand dog-leg, tee the ball lower than normal. The lower tee will cause you to hit down slightly making it easier to hit a controlled fade. Swing slightly out-to-in. Use a driver or a 1-iron as it is easier to hit a fade with a straight-faced club

Conversely, short shots are very difficult to bend left to right since the extra loft and open clubface creates backspin as opposed to side-spin. In normal circumstances then, if for some reason you need to shape shots, it is much easier to fade long shots (straight-faced clubs) and draw short shots (the lofted clubs).

The lie of the ball has a specific bearing on what type of shot is easiest. A tight lie requires a steep swing to create a solid impact. This type of action encourages an open clubface at impact and therefore a fade is the right shot to picture from this type of lie. Conversely, when the ball is sitting up in soft grass this encourages a sweeping action which tends to close the clubface and therefore a draw is the natural shape shot.

Sloping lies produce automatic impact conditions. When the ball is below the feet, the club is bound to swing on a more upright arc which tends to create an open clubface at impact, so a fade should be allowed for. When the ball is above the feet, a shallower in-to-in hitting area closes the club so this time allow for a draw.

How to play dog-legs
In playing dog-legs, those holes that bend to the right from the tee are best approached with the ball teed somewhat lower than normal for the driver. The lower tee will automatically create a slight downward blow, and the straightness of the clubface making contact on the back of the ball makes it easy to fade. Holes that bend to the left and call for a draw are often best tackled by using a lofted wood. A draw requires the clubface to be closed at impact. With the driver you have very little margin for error and unless your natural shot is a draw with a driver it is always far easier and much safer to play this shot with the 3-wood.

Playing in crosswinds really can test all of us. In a right-to-left wind with shots to the green, over-club and swing easily. This will tend to leave the clubface open and therefore counteract the wind. In a left-to-right

When trying for a draw around a left-hand dog-leg, tee the ball higher than for a fade and use a lofted wood, not the driver. It is easier and safer than the driver which has very little room for error. To get the draw the clubface must be closed slightly at impact. Swing in-to-out

wind it is often better to under-club and hit hard which will tend to close the clubface at impact, again counteracting the wind. Tee shots in a crosswind for the most part should simply be set off on the windward side allowing for the wind to bring the ball back. This way the wind is being used to attain distance as opposed to those shots to the green when the wind is deliberately counteracted in order for the ball to stop.

While all the above is true, most of us have our own favourite shot in which we have confidence. However, this advice should help you not to play the wrong shot at the wrong time. Therefore remember the following:

1 The straighter the club the easier to fade.
2 Do not attempt to draw the driver unless you do it naturally.
3 When the lie is tight, play a fade.
4 Do not attempt to draw the ball unless the lie is good.
5 Do not attempt to fade the short irons.

How to combat uneven lies

Do you ever stop and ponder why you mishit the last shot? Was it through a bad swing, some distraction or was it because you were playing from an uneven lie and did not have the experience through lack of practice from a similar situation?

You see it every day: whenever golfers go out to practise, the first thing they do is find some even piece of turf. Who can blame them? After all, they have gone there to correct some fault, to practise to maintain standards, or play better shots, and we all get our best results hitting shots from ideal lies.

There is no doubt about it that striking the ball from level ground is sensible and a help towards producing a good swing. However, the hard facts are that you can only be sure during a round of having eighteen good even lies on the tees from which you will be playing.

Have you ever stopped to consider how many times during a round of golf you will encounter a flat fairway lie? A low-handicap man, who will be playing fewer shots anyway than the high handicapper, will not have more than, on average, one-third of his fairway shots from even lies – at most, six or seven shots per round. Yet nearly every golfer seems to overlook the fact that so much of his golf will be from less-than-perfect positions.

In general terms, during play, no conscious notice is registered when negotiating slight slopes or undulations – one foot an inch or so above the other and so on. Nature will compensate automatically and make adjustments.

Carry out the following test for yourself. Set yourself up to play a shot with an open stance – left foot up to four inches back from the right foot – with your shoulders parallel to the intended line of flight. Once at that address position, and after a 'waggle' or two to get really relaxed, stop for a moment and then look down at your knees.

Although your feet are in an open position, the knees are likely to be parallel to the intended line of flight. Your left leg will be bent a little more than the right leg. All this happened because nature dictated the correct posture and balance.

The same holds true when adopting a shut stance – right foot back from the left foot – with the shoulders square to target line. This time, of course, it will be the right leg that is bent more than the left leg, but the knees remain parallel to the intended line of flight.

These responsive movements can be compared with what happens when you walk up a hill. Without acting consciously you lean forwards to maintain balance – to centralize your centre of gravity but walking downhill you tend to lean backwards.

Here is another example: when walking along a hillslope you lean towards the hill. With the slope going from left to right your right leg will be quite straight and your left leg will be partly bent. Obviously the reverse happens when walking in the other direction. Now, if these things can happen instinctively during everyday life, why do we golfers make such a fuss about uphill, downhill and across lies? And why practise continually from level land when so many

When playing from an uneven lie with shoulders square to the target, your knees will follow suit regardless of your stance

uneven shots are bound to be in demand in a normal game?

It is sensible during your practice sessions to spend a little time – do not overdo it because it could alter your swing permanently – learning how best to play from awkward lies. You will also get experience of how the flight of the ball is affected.

Most slopes during play go unnoticed but there are some that are quite severe. Many of these are experienced while playing on seaside courses, when quite often we get more than our fair share. Links courses, like St Andrews and Royal

When playing awkward shots natural balance will set your knees parallel to the line of the shoulders, at address and impact

When playing from an uphill lie, try to make the clubhead follow the line of the slope at the start of the backswing and through the impact area

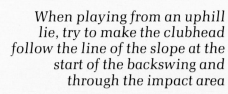

St George's in Great Britain, readily come to mind.

For those who like to have detail in their mind when tackling *exaggerated* uneven lies here is some advice about playing the ball on five different types of slope. Before going into such detail there is one thing that applies to all of them and this is the most important thing. The natural posture adopted when negotiating a shot from a slope will dictate the shape of your swing. Do not fight the sort of swing that your stance will produce. You are going to get a certain shaped shot from different lies – whether it be a slice or a hook – and you should learn to recognize this.

If circumstances dictate that you are likely to slice, or hook, play a high or low flying ball, then do not try to

adapt your swing to neutralize the prospect. Far better to acknowledge the likely flight that can be expected and allow for it.

It is important, too, when playing from a noticeable slope, to accept the fact that your length of swing – back and through – and the distance achieved will be curtailed somewhat, the amount naturally depending on the severity of the undulation.

The uphill shot

We shall start with the uphill shot with the ball already at rest on the slope. Nature will tell you to have your right leg straight and your left knee bent. The weight will be mainly on the right foot, and the right shoulder much lower than usual. The ball will be positioned, in general

terms, midway between the left foot and the middle of stance.

From such a stance you will be hitting the ball more on the upswing causing it to fly higher than usual. This means that the ball will not travel as far as when playing from level ground. Nature is turning, say, a 5-iron into a 6-, 7- or even an 8-iron.

So if the uphill distance should indicate a 5-iron then take out of the bag a 4- or 3-iron. On occasions a 4-wood held down the grip could be the answer to your problem.

Take into consideration, too, that because your left leg is bent more than usual due to the slope it will restrict the length of both the back and the through swing. The thing you need to concentrate on during your swing is trying to make the clubhead follow the line of the slope – the result being that, for iron or wood shots, you will be making (naturally within limits) a normal backswing.

Through the impact area you do not want to dig the clubface into the ground, and the answer is to keep the clubhead moving up the line of the slope. The danger is that as the weight is so much on the right foot to neutralize the slope, the player can lose his balance easily during the swing causing him either to lean or fall back. Watch out for this trap and try to keep as steady as possible throughout the action.

It is common to pull this shot to the left so allow for it and aim off to the right. How much you aim off target is governed by the severity of slope.

The downhill shot

Downhill lie problems are reversed

How to combat uneven lies

and the main weight is now on the left leg, with the right knee bent more than is customary. The best position for the ball during this shot is from the centre of the stance to around half way back towards the right foot. Such generalization depends largely on the individual and steepness of the slope. It moves the bottom part of the swing arc back into this area.

You will get a steeper backswing and once again on returning to the ball make the clubhead follow the line of the slope as much as possible.

From downhill lies you will experience a lower flying shot so now you can drop down a club or two. If a 6-iron would seem correct then take out a 7-iron, and so forth.

The biggest danger is topping. This is due to the natural reaction to sway down the slope just before impact. Even playing correctly on a downhill lie you may experience a slight fade or even a slice, so it will not hurt to make some adjustment and aim a little to the left.

Standing below the ball
Now for standing below the ball – the first of the cross slopes – with the ball above the level of your feet. To stop you standing too upright, hold the club a little lower down the grip. Position yourself to the ball so that it is more or less central at address. The weight will be divided between both feet but automatically back towards the heels.

The swing plane will be flatter than usual and the tendency will be to draw or hook the ball to the left. So anticipate it and set yourself up at address aiming a little right of target.

More often than not, this allowance pays off. Keeping your hands slightly ahead of the clubface during the swing will help you to minimize the expected draw.

As you will be holding the club somewhat down the shaft, distance will be reduced, and to compensate it will be necessary to use one or two clubs stronger than otherwise.

Standing above the ball
When standing above the ball you face a more difficult shot because as you are standing above the level of the ball you may feel that you are going to topple forward on to it when you are swinging.

Position the ball opposite a midway point between the feet, and as you will have to reach for the ball you must stand a shade closer than routine. It also helps to bend the knees more than normal. Hold the club at full length and have the hands just a bit in front of the ball at address with the weight back towards the heels. A fade or slice is in prospect so you will find it helpful to close the clubface a little but make sure you do this before taking up your grip.

Nature will insist that your backswing becomes more upright than it was before, and your backswing (and the throughswing) will definitely be restricted – do not fight this. Accept the fact that you will lose distance and use a more powerful club than perhaps you might think you need.

To offset that expected slice or fade, aim somewhat to the left. The amount of slice can vary quite a lot. The slice happens because it is difficult to hit straight through the ball and it is far

easier, unfortunately, due to the awkward stance, to swing the clubhead on a track from out-to-in across the target line.

Combined downhill and side slopes
This is a difficult one when you find a downhill lie coupled with the ball being below the feet. Socketing is not uncommon from this situation. The reason for this is that anxiety creeps in and makes most golfers tense up and grip too tightly. When this happens, free swinging is exchanged for a stiff-like action and the player sways forwards and sideways along the ground slope. The clubhead is then pushed right into the ball – hence causing the shank.

At address, have the ball positioned just right of centre. As the weight will fall mainly on the left foot, so the left leg will be straightish and the right knee bent. You will find the weight also moving towards your toes. Because it is partly a downhill lie you will achieve more distance than usual so select a club less powerful than otherwise required.

You do not want to swing too upright so keep the clubhead low to the ground as far as possible on the backswing and throughswing. Put another way, try to keep the clubhead following the slope of the ground.

There you have the most common of the awkward lies and how best to combat them, and remember, as explained, that the ball is more than likely to travel off line. Accept that fact and do not attempt to change your swing in the hope of hitting straight on target – far better to make allowances while lining up.

1

2

When playing from a downhill lie(1), your weight will be on the left foot. The right leg will have to be bent more to compensate. Position the ball further back in the stance with hands ahead of the ball

When playing a shot from above the level of your feet(2) you can expect a flatter backswing. This will cause a draw or hook so allow for this by aiming right of the target at address

3

4

When above the ball(3) stand closer than usual with the ball centred in the stance. You will have a more upright backswing than normal from which you will fade the ball. So aim left with a slightly closed clubface at address

From a combined downhill and side slope(4) it is very difficult to play an accurate shot. Allow for the expected fade or slice and try to follow the slope with the clubhead at the start of the swing and through impact

How to play from poor lies

You will not get the ball out of a divot mark and flying with a straight-faced club. Resist the temptation to use any club more powerful than a 7-iron. Should the divot mark be quite deep, then consider taking a 9-iron or even a wedge. Always use a club with plenty of loft on it.

The correct position for the shot is to stand with the ball in the centre of the stance, or even back towards the right foot. This brings the hands in front of the clubhead which, in turn, promotes a steeper backswing than normal. You can then chop down on the ball and move it from the rut. It is less of a proper swing, more a stab shot, with little or no follow-through– if you like, squirting the ball out.

A lot of run can be expected as the ball will come out low if struck steeply and cleanly. Should the ball lie at rest at the start of the divot mark then you will have to take turf first.

Why no more than a 7-iron? Standing in front of the ball with the hands also in front reduces the loft on the clubface.

Tight for a bare lie
These should not really present a lot of problems but for the average-handicap golfer they do. When faced with a close lie a player freezes and mentally accepts that a poor shot from such a lie is inevitable.

This is negative thinking, but after putting the following instruction into practice you will be pleasantly surprised to find that a close lie will no longer be the hazard you have always recognized.

When playing from a close lie, steeper downswing is required to get the ball up and away, but do not consciously try to do this as there is a danger of exaggerating the movement.

All you need do is position yourself at address so that the ball is almost central in the stance with the hands slightly forward of the ball, and the clubface square to the intended line of flight. Automatically, this affects the backswing by making it more upright than normal from which a steeper downswing will result. At impact the ball will then be hit down, squeezing it between clubface and turf and driving it forward and up.

Naturally the ball will fly lower than is usual for the club being used, so allow for some run after landing. A more lofted club to compensate is the answer. However, to play a delicate pitch shot from a tight lie over a green-side bunker or some other obstacle, when the flagstick is near the hazard, is a difficult one. You need to bite into the turf so use a sharp-soled club such as a 9-iron. Unlike the longer shots from a similar lie, play the ball this time well *left* of centre. The feet and shoulders should be in an open position and the stance narrow. Hold the club down the grip somewhat for finer control with the clubface slightly open to the target line and the hands ahead of the ball.

As for the swing, it must be short, slow, deliberate and travelling along a track parallel to the feet line (out-to-in). Keeping the hands in front of the

To hit down steeply when playing from a divot mark, your hands should be well in front of the clubhead, the ball positioned off the right side

From a bare lie, to produce an upright backswing and steeper downswing, the ball should be central to the stance, clubface square to the target

For a short shot over an obstacle from a tight lie, use a sharp-soled lofted club. Open the face and stance, the ball off the left side

For a ball plugged in sand, adopt a slightly open stance, the ball just left of centre and the club-face square. Hit down and through

For a ball on the edge of a fair-way bunker use a sharp-bladed club. Open the face and swing steeply down behind the ball

clubhead with little or no wrist action will offset any tendency that you may have to scoop the ball up and over the hazard. The loft on the clubface does that for you so do not quit on the shot.

Plugged in bunker

The only way to get the ball out is by taking plenty of sand, and to do that a firm grip is the first priority. Adopt a slightly open stance (left foot about one inch back from the right foot) and 'dig' the feet well in to get a firm footing. Have the ball positioned only a fraction left of centre.

The hands should be opposite the ball with the clubface square to target, but should the ball be deeply buried turn the clubface in a little so that it looks to be aiming a little left of the intended line. This will help neutralize the reverse turning of the club-head on impact with the sand.

You will need to chop down into the sand close behind the ball and to achieve this the backswing must be on a much steeper plane than normal. It is not a traditional swing and some force has to be used. Swing the club a

little from out-to-in and parallel to the feet line keeping your hands in front of the clubhead throughout the action. It may be difficult but try hard to follow right through. Never leave the clubhead buried in the sand after making the stroke. You cannot expect to play a precision shot and it is reward enough to get the ball out.

Edge of bunker

You are close to the green and the ball has just tipped over into sand. There is a small ledge between the fairway and the ball, and you have one foot on the grass and the other in sand.

Use a sharp-bladed club, 9-iron or wedge, open the clubface and take an upright backswing. Hit steeply down into the turf at the side of the bunker and try to follow through if possible. It is a difficult shot and to get the ball on the green represents success.

Off a gravel path

Prepare to play a stiff-wristed shot from the middle of the stance, and feel that you are almost going to top the shot. In fact, what you do is try to

hit the ball with a flattish arc just below centre. Avoid hitting the ground – if only to save your club – and for the ordinary player the shot is a half-swing. You will have limited follow-through and the result should be a low flying shot with a lot of run.

Playing from the rough

First, some general advice for those of you who have problems playing these shots. The most common mistake is trying to make up distance after an initial error. Too many players succumb to temptation and risk a power-ful club such as a 3-iron or 4-wood.

Unfortunately, escaping from the rough using one of the power clubs occasionally succeeds and the player having achieved it, say one time in thirty, remembers only that single success, forgets the twenty nine disasters, and stubbornly will not accept the inevitable.

Much better to accept the fact that you have probably lost a shot than to drop two or three attempting the near impossible. After all, having returned to the fairway it is still possible to get

How to play from poor lies

close to the pin with your third or fourth shot and have a chance of a single putt for par.

When in medium or deep rough it makes sense to get the ball back into play by the shortest route. Take, for example, the instance when you are in the rough and 190 yards from the green – a difficult shot at that distance even if you were on the fairway.

Your chances therefore from out of rough are virtually nil so forget your big clubs. When playing from the rough there is always a danger of the clubhead turning over (closing) at impact. It smothers the shot and the ball invariably flies low and to the left. The reason? As the club approaches impact the hosel and shaft get tangled up with the grass which turns the clubhead. To counteract this, address the ball with the clubface somewhat open and adopt a firm grip, especially with the left hand.

In addition, there is a cushioning effect of grass between the clubface and ball resulting in loss of control and reduced backspin. Such effects are very noticeable when playing from greenside rough. The smooth surface of the green is unable to hold the ball, whether it is high flying or low flying, and even tends to exaggerate the shot's runaway tendency.

If the rough is wet and the ball is lying quite well you have to guard against a 'flier' (a ball that flies further than it normally would for the same club and virtually out of control). This is caused by the wet grass coming in contact with the club first and producing a skidding effect – the wet grass between clubface and ball acting like grease. How to avoid a

Severiano Ballesteros plays a 'pop' shot from rough by the edge of the green

Graham Marsh lets the clubhead do the work on this shot from semi-rough

flier? A punch shot (which will not give sure control) is the only solution when the ball is in wet rough.

Semi-rough
This is the least of your problems and while a longish club may be possible you should always use a more lofted club than the one suitable from the fairway. Remember, the ball will run more when played from the rough.

Imagine a 5-iron fairway shot. The same ball in the rough would require a 7-iron, and with the extra run you are more than likely to finish with the same distance.

In wet conditions you need to guard against a 'flier' so position the ball midway in the stance with the clubface square to the intended line. Take a three-quarter backswing and punch the ball forward. The follow-through will be shorter than usual for the same club. Expect quite a bit of run after the ball lands.

Should you be near the green in semi-rough, use a lofted club. Position yourself so that the ball is central in the stance and hold the club down the grip. Now, keeping your hands in front of the clubhead, play a sharp 'stab and stop' shot.

Medium-rough
It all depends this time whether the ball is lying down or sitting up. Both shots have to be treated with care. If the ball is right down in the roots of

Jack Nicklaus demonstrates his power as he recovers from thick rough

Tom Watson extricates himself from some of Royal Birkdale's savage rough during the 1983 Open Championship

the grass then the only solution is to take a very lofted club such as a 9-iron or a wedge. Adopt a slightly more open stance with the ball positioned towards the right foot. Use a more upright backswing and hit down on the ball. You have to accept some loss of distance.

When the ball is sitting up, it becomes possible to use a straighter-faced club, say, as much as a 4-iron. This time position the ball left side of centre in the stance as you will need to sweep the ball away. Take plenty of time over this shot and make sure that you do not go underneath the ball or it will be ballooned.

Deep-rough or fern

The only alternative you have here is whether you choose to use a wedge or a sand iron. Always reach for the heaviest club in the bag. Do not be greedy. Instead, settle for getting out of trouble even if it means playing out of the rough sideways.

Getting the ball back into play must be your first concern. Force the ball out rather than attempting a delicately judged stroke.

To get the best possible results when playing from such rough you will need to reduce the inevitable tangling of the clubhead and shaft with the long grass or tall fern during the backswing and downswing. To achieve this you must have the ball positioned right of centre after adopting an open stance. Take a steep backswing and strike the ball a descending blow with the hands ahead of the clubface. Naturally with this 'chopping' action there is little or even no follow-through.

Heather

When this type of growth has been cut short it is very misleading and often looks as if you can take a long club with confidence. However, this usually proves disastrous.

The ball looks to be sitting up beautifully but the 'branch stems' usually turn the clubhead right round and stop it dead. Utmost caution is necessary. Never go lower than a 5-iron even if the distance would seem to require a 3-wood. When in thick heather, play the shot as you would from deep-rough.

Thick clover

Should the ball be buried in this 'mushy' weed you will need to hit strongly through the shot and force the ball out. Use the same method as when playing from medium-rough.

At times you may find the ball lying in thin clover on the fairway where the mower has failed to cut because of some small ridge or undulation guarding the area. Do not be deceived by this seemingly fair lie. The reason? Invariably a ball hit out of clover will run after it lands because its soft stems and leaves have got between the clubface and the ball and reduced backspin. So always take one club less than you think you require to allow for the additional run.

Finally, before playing from any type of rough always take a note of which way the grass or stems are lying. When they are bent towards the target, address the ball well left of centre with the clubhead above ground – as you would in a bunker. This will help stop the rough interfering with the clubhead at the start of the backswing.

If the rough is lying away from the target – against the run of play – you must expect a lot of grass or similar, between the clubhead and ball at impact. This is unavoidable and not unlike when playing an explosion shot from sand when the clubhead does not make direct contact with the ball. Because of this cushioning effect between the clubface and ball, little distance and control can be expected.

In general terms, depending on the thickness of the rough, you will need to play this shot from the centre of the stance, use a steeper backswing and hit harder than usual. Experience here is the best teacher.

For all the poor lie shots there is one golden rule: whatever the circumstances the main object is to get the ball back into play.

Getting out of trouble

Even the greatest tournament players of our time all find trouble of some sort during virtually any round of golf. These, remember, are the experts with the luxury of being able to practise continually to eliminate any errors.

Now if they can get into trouble while knocking the ball round 6,800 yards, how much more likely will it be that you will stand with a furrowed brow looking down on one of the game's infuriating problem shots?

Thus we must all expect, either through a playing mistake or sheer bad luck, to experience these undesirable encounters of a close kind.

Winning, most decidedly, is more about being able to play the good recovery shot than it is about being fairly consistent around the course. If you can get yourself adequately back into play then you always have a chance of making par.

We all want to avoid trouble areas but if you will allow overwhelming caution to dominate then you will play every shot with a negative approach. Who dares wins! What we need is a balanced assessment of potential danger and the likelihood of golfing success.

Most club golfers leave the course trying to analyze the swing error that caused them to hit at least two or three of the bad shots that found trouble in their round — usually very conscious of how many shots they dropped through having to play from the difficult places.

The first piece of advice is not to analyze the reason for a particular bad shot, unless the error is a regular part of your game. Trouble is inevitable

With the ball in the centre of your stance, this brings your hands in front of the clubhead, which leads to a steeper backswing. Chop down on the ball with a punch-type shot with a three-quarter swing and the hands forward of the clubhead throughout with little follow-through

Always have a few practice swings to help get the feel. Stroke the putt and never give it a sharp tap on fast greens (illustration). With the blade at right angles to the chosen line, swing the putter low back and low through with a controlled stroke (photo)

and you will find it more profitable to learn to play the trouble shots with competence.

Ball in a divot mark

One of the most common problems is one that we all know and one that can be found even after a cracking shot. You walk up the fairway happily until you arrive to find the ball lying in a divot. Try to leave on one side the mental feeling that this is all so unfair. Whoever claimed that golf was a fair game, anyway? What you have to do now is to concentrate more on getting the ball out and flying towards the target.

You will not do that with a straight-faced club – and leave the woods in the bag. Do not be tempted to take any club more powerful than a 6-iron. If the divot mark is quite deep you may have to consider a 9-iron or even a wedge. Whatever your choice, always make sure that the club has an attractive amount of loft on it.

Loft is essential because the correct position at address is to have the ball in the centre of your stance, or possibly back towards the right foot. Automatically this brings the hands in front of the clubhead, and this leads to a steeper backswing than normal. You do not have to think about that because it is a completely natural response.

You can then chop it down at the back of the ball and move it from the rut. A punch-type shot, rather than a proper swing, is required. It is a three-quarter swing with the hands forward of the clubhead throughout. There is little or no follow-through.

Expect the shot to fly low and the

ball to run on after it lands. You will have struck steeply and cleanly, but when the ball rests at the far end of the divot mark (where the turf can almost form a step) you will need to hit down steeply and take earth before the ball. Hit the back of the ball first and then you can easily drive it into the 'step'.

A final word of explanation. Why draw the line at the 6-iron? It is because the hands are in front of the ball right through the action and this reduces the loft of the club.

Treacherous downhill putts

The next poser is how to finish close to the pin when faced with a treach-

erous downhill putt. This is the most delicate of shots and, above all, requires feel: that is, feel of distance and clubhead movement.

Obviously you will study the part of the green involved carefully: the line, texture of grass, area immediately around the hole, and 'nap' or 'grain' (the direction in which the blades of grass grow), etc. This should give you some idea of what the ball will do as it loses momentum, and the strength needed to 'die' at the hole. Lee Trevino is a good example to follow. He always studies the putt from all angles, almost like an animal stalking its prey.

The best method in order to feel

Getting out of trouble

distance is to stroke a putt, but always have a few practice swings to help with this feel. *Never* give it a sharp tap on fast greens. You can usually control a stroking action but not the 'rap' method.

Try not to leave a fast downhill putt short. If it runs past the hole, then at least you will have given the hole a chance with the added advantage of an uphill putt back.

When faced with a short, curly two-foot putt, liable to borrow, make up your mind to be courageous and hit it firmly into the back of the hole. If it misses you are likely to be in trouble but practice will make perfect and your chances of sinking a firm putt are better than when trying to coddle it in. This is something that you will have to find out for yourself through experience.

On a long downhill slope, where the surface is like glass, it is best to trickle or finesse the ball towards the hole. Of course it is chancy and you will need a share of luck, no matter how nicely you play the shot. You can help your prospects by making sure that the putter blade is at right angles to the chosen line you wish the ball to follow and that you keep your head steady when stroking the putt. Never change your mind during the action, or rhythm is lost... and swing the putter low back and low through, near to the turf.

Ball plugged in a bunker
Headache number three is when the ball is well buried or plugged in a bunker. It could be a bunker full of wet sand, or it might be one containing soft, dry sand.

Dig your feet well into the sand (photo left). If the ball is well-buried, close the clubface slightly to offset the turning as the clubhead strikes the sand (illustration). Follow right through (photo right) and never leave the clubhead buried in the sand after the strike

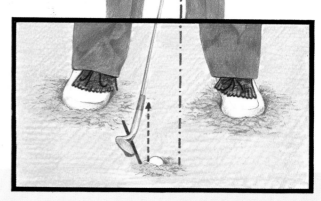

When you have to keep the ball low, a sharp stab shot with a 4-, 5- or 6-iron is needed. Direction is more important than length (illustration). Keep the hands in front of the clubhead at address and at all times through the shot (photo)

The advice is much the same for both circumstances except that in wet and firm sand it might be advisable to take a sharp-edged club such as a 9-iron to help cut through the sand. In normal conditions use the sand-iron, but the rest of the instruction is unchanged.

When a ball is buried you cannot get it out unless you take sand. To do that a firm grip is the priority. Adopt a slightly open stance with the left foot about an inch or so back from the right foot. Make sure you dig your feet well in to obtain a firm footing and in so doing you get an idea of the texture of the sand – this is important.

Remember that you are dealing with a buried or plugged ball, and the instruction will be somewhat different when the problem is that of the normal bunker shot.

Have the ball either in the centre of stance or a fraction right of centre. The hands should be ahead of the ball with the clubface square to target, but if the ball is fiendishly buried, close the clubface a little so that it seems to be aiming slightly left of the intended line. This closed face approach helps to dig the ball out and neutralize the turning of the clubhead on impact with the sand.

What you must do is chop down on the sand close behind the ball, and to achieve this make the backswing much more steep than is customary. It is a 'one-off' swing and some force has to be used. It may be difficult but try hard to follow right through, and never leave the clubhead buried in the sand after making the stroke.

Swing the club a little from out-to-in and parallel to the feet line, keep-ing your hands in front of the clubhead during the action. It is impossible to play a precision shot but the reward is to get back on to grass.

Through the gap

Now to the problem of firing a shot through a narrow gap between trees or obstacles. What you must do is take your time and weigh up the situation carefully. If the gap is too narrow and the odds too heavily against, then a sideways or even backwards shot is the sensible course of action.

However, if you have decided that you have a reasonable chance of negotiating the gap, pick out the largest gap available rather than letting the direction of the hole dictate tactics. You know that the more lofted the club used, the quicker the ball will rise. It is much better if the shot stays low.

What is needed is a sharp stab shot with a 4-, 5- or 6-iron – naturally the height required governs the choice of club. Direction is more important than length. Take care that you are lined up correctly, clubface square to the intended line, and if it helps pick out a spot that you want the clubhead to travel over. The hands are ahead of the ball at address and throughout – this reduces clubface loft.

Because you are using a stiff stabbing action there is the danger of swaying in the same direction as the clubhead is travelling, which will cause the shot to be topped. To help eliminate this possibility, have a few practice swings before you actually play the shot.

When you meet the problem of playing out from under a bush or trees with branches brushing the ground, grip further down the shaft. You will have to settle, with a 4- or 5-iron, for a short stabbing action. Hold the club firmly and try to keep the hands leading the clubhead at all times during the shot.

The correct way to hook and slice

There are occasions during any round of golf when you may find yourself faced with a situation where you need to bend a shot round a tree or similar obstruction. Other times you may want to bend the shot away from a beckoning out-of-bounds area, or hold the ball against a strong crosswind. To be able to play such shots, at will, you must have the knowledge of how to hook and slice the ball.

Ask the club golfer how to play an intentional hook shot and the likelihood is that he will tell you to close the stance – that is, to have the left foot in advance of the right.

As far as stance is concerned that is not the way to hook the ball. The moment the player closes his stance he will automatically lock his left hip from turning out of the way in response to the clubhead as it nears impact. When this happens the clubhead will not have a free passage through the ball. The hands will arrive in front of the clubhead at impact and the probable result is a push shot out to the right of the target.

Better advice would have been to slightly 'toe-in' the clubface at address with the ball positioned towards right of centre in the stance and move the hands round somewhat to the right on the grip. How much you move the hands round will depend on the amount of hook requir-

To play a hook adopt a slightly open stance. Close the shoulders, position the ball right of centre in the stance, point the toe of the club inwards, and move the hands round to the right side of the club

The address position for achieving a hook will produce a flatter backswing and an exaggerated in-to-out swing path. Together with the shut clubface, this will start the ball out to the right. As the ball starts to lose momentum the side-spin imparted at impact will cause the ball to move to the left towards the end of its flight. Here a 6-iron is used to hit the ball a 4-iron distance

To play a slice adopt an open stance and shoulder position. Now position the ball towards the left foot, leave the clubface open at address, and move the hands to the left on the club and keep them in front of the club-head throughout the swing action

The address position for achieving a slice will produce an upright backswing and an out-to-in swing path. The ball will start out to the left, but will gradually drift to the right. The clockwise spin causes the ball to lose distance, so here a 4-iron is being used

ed. Open the stance a few degrees and close the shoulders to the intended line of flight.

The altered grip coupled with the 'toed-in' clubface position at address will ensure a shut face at impact, while the closed shoulders and ball position help to flatten the back-swing along a definite inside track. This, in turn, sets up an exaggerated swing path through the ball going from in-to-out.

As the clubhead comes into the hit-ting area the moderately open stance will allow the left hip to readily turn out of the way in response to the club-head travelling through. The shot will start out to the right and then hook back into play due to the anti-clockwise spin imparted to the ball by the closed clubface at impact.

Make sure when playing for an intentional hook to select a less powerful club than one you would use for a normal shot for the same distance. The closed clubface delofts a club and turns, for example, the loft

of a 6-iron into a 4-iron. Add to that the run on the ball that can be expected from a hooked shot.

The layman will tell you also that the correct way to play an intended fade or slice is just to open the stance (left foot back from the right). That may help to some degree, but more often than not a pulled shot straight to the left will result.

Keep the hands ahead

The best advice when a fade or slice is wanted is to open the clubface very slightly at address with the ball posi-tioned opposite a point just inside the left heel. Then move the hands round a little to the left on the club; you can increase this grip alteration when a lot of slice is in demand. At the same time, open the stance and shoulders. Have the hands ahead of the ball, keeping them that way throughout the action.

This grip on the club keeps the clubface open throughout impact, helped by the hands being kept in

front of the clubhead throughout the swing. The open stance and ball position, along with the shoulder line, will provide a more upright backswing giving a swing track from out-to-in across the line of flight, imparting spin on the ball. The shot will start out to the left with clock-wise spin. When the forward thrust starts to weaken, the spin imparted at impact takes over and the ball curls to the right.

You will need to use a less-lofted club for the distance involved, because the open clubface together with the out-to-in swing track auto-matically weakens shot power.

Spend some of your practice time playing the intentional hook and slice. Then you will be prepared to play such shots that might be in demand when playing the course. Remember that a shot executed a number of times goes into the memory bank to be used when called upon.

How to combat the advancing years

When the body becomes less supple and pivoting is difficult, it is very easy to develop an out-to-in swing which gives you far too steep an angle of approach to the ball

The greatest strength of golf is the handicapping system whereby players of differing ability can compete with each other on equal terms. As you get older, you will find that you do not play quite as well as you did in your youth, but you *can* still enjoy the game to the full.

To know your limitations when playing golf is of the utmost importance irrespective of how well you play. The older you become, the more vital it is to come to terms with your deficiencies and to readjust your sights accordingly.

The long par four holes are usually the first holes where golfers may experience problems and it is no good thinking that what was, in the past, a drive and a medium iron can be reached with the same club twenty years later. Only vexation ensues if you adopt this misguided attitude.

As your body becomes less supple, it is all too easy to fall into incorrect swing habits. It is easy also to recognize these habits and take measures against them. Therefore, adjustments must be made when the body resists the complete pivot which is so essential for a proper swing. You still have to position the club correctly in the backswing so as to deliver the clubhead squarely into the back of the ball as always.

Since the ball is positioned to the side of you the swing path needs to be from the inside to straight through in order that the club should approach the ball on a shallow arc with the clubface squaring up at impact. This application will maximize distance whatever your clubhead speed. Few people understand that an out-to-in swing is so damaging because of the steepish angle at which the club approaches the ball.

If, therefore, it is important to hit from the inside even when pivoting is more difficult, it is of real benefit to position the ball further back in the stance or more towards the right foot. This makes it easy to close the body position. There should be a conscious turning of the hips so that they face more behind the ball at address. This position also tends to strengthen the grip which means that both hands will be turned more over the shaft.

The awareness, at address, of the correct swing path into the ball should lead to much more of the effort coming from the hands and arms and much less from the body. At the same time, the change of grip will help deliver the clubface squarely.

The short game

The area of the game that does not require clubhead speed – the short game – should receive particular attention since it is in this department that shots can be made up and practice can be of real benefit. Much of our time and effort over the years has been spent hitting the ball a long way but once you recognize that huge distances are no longer attainable, the desire to practise the short game can often lead to some improvement in this very important department.

Certain adjustments in equipment can also be an advantage. The long irons with their lack of loft and poker-like feel do require good clubhead speed to be played succesfully. A 5-wood should, with its extra loft and greater feel, take the place of the 2-

and 3-irons. The driver should also have sufficient loft to put the ball in the air easily since the positioning of the ball further back in the stance will tend to de-loft the club. Lighter clubs are beneficial as we get older. Anything too heavy leads to the body taking over as opposed to the hands and arms applying the clubhead to the ball.

To make sure you bring the club into the ball from the inside a simple adjustment in your stance is necessary. Move the ball back towards your right foot and at the same time make a conscious effort to turn your hips so that they face behind the ball at address. This helps to strengthen your grip, making it easier to deliver the clubhead squarely

The point of practice

The handicapping system is one of golf's greatest features, as stated before, for it enables players of varying competence to enjoy a round together. The game is there to be played but if you wish to play better, practice is essential.

However, there is practice and practice. To simply hit as many balls as possible without thought and application will not do much other than to groove any mistakes that are already present in your game.

A competent professional, in a lesson, will diagnose mistakes and show how to eradicate them. He will prove his skill by getting the pupil, during the course of the lesson, to hit better shots. However, habit is a very difficult thing to overcome and the only permanent way is by correct and constant practice.

Clear concept essential

For those of you who enjoy practice and who are striving for improvement, a clear mental concept is essential before you start. It is equally important that the muscles are in a fit condition before the first balls are hit, otherwise the first few shots will not be good and the whole session will get off to a bad start.

Swinging a weighted club, or, more conveniently, taking two or three iron clubs together has two major benefits. It loosens the back muscles and helps to create the right tempo. Another appropriate exercise is to slip a club across the back with the arms behind the club. It is important, however, when doing this exercise, not to point each end of the club, when pivoting, to where the ball will be since that type of shoulder pivot would be far too steep. Take up the normal address position and pivot the shoulders, pointing the shaft at the ground some fifteen to twenty yards ahead of you.

Swinging any club normally, without a ball, should be repeated some ten to twenty times before the first ball is struck. Many players would claim to have a good practice swing but, of course, since there is no ball, there is no proof of the validity of this claim. The point is that without a ball, although the swing may look good, unless the clubface is square on impact, a shot with a ball will not be very effective. To practise swinging, pick some particular spot on the ground and endeavour to hit it. This spot, where the club reaches the bottom of its arc, should be varied, from the same stance, in order to create the necessary precision allied to the free-swinging motion is that easily achieved without a ball, since there is no element of fear.

Since the correct set-up, meaning clubhead, aim and body position, is so vital to good striking, it is essential to hit shots to a target. Lay two clubs on the ground, parallel to each other, so that the clubface and the foot alignment can be checked easily. It must be remembered that not only the feet need to be in position but, more importantly, the upper half of the body, too. The shoulders and hips should also be parallel to the line of aim.

By far the greatest proportion of golfers tend to slice the ball. This is

Sam Torrance practises under the watchful eye of his father, Bob

Swinging a weighted club, or, more conveniently, taking two or three iron clubs together has two major benefits. It loosens the back muscles and helps to create the right tempo. Another appropriate exercise is to slip a club across the back with the arm behind the club. It is important, however, when doing this exercise, not to point each end of the club when pivoting to where the ball will

Right   **Wrong**

be since that type of shoulder pivot would be far too steep.
Take up the normal address position and pivot the shoulders, pointing the shaft at the ground some fifteen to twenty yards ahead of you

By far the greatest proportion of golfers tend to slice the ball. This is usually a result of overuse of the body with under-use of the hands and arms. The best practice for curing this type of mistake is to hit shots, using a medium iron with the feet together. From this narrow base, overuse of the body is immediately restricted

usually a result of over-use of the body with under-use of the hands and arms. The very best practice for this type of mistake is to hit shots with a 6-iron, with the feet together. From this narrow base, over-use of the body is immediately restricted, since an instant lack of balance will be felt. The thinking should be of the club being in the target direction at the top of the backswing, using your normal length of swing from where it is swung through the ball predominantly with the hands and arms.

From the inside

Do *not* practise full shots into a left-to-right wind. The position of the ball relative to the player means that the club should swing into the ball from the inside in order to release the club-face straight and square into the back of the ball. A left-to-right wind makes this movement very difficult to achieve, so even if this entails a considerable walk, hit balls against the wind or into a right-to-left wind. If you are working on your full swing, use a relatively easy club. A 6-iron is an easy club to use and yet needs a fairly full swing. Alternatively, use a no. 4-wood. For most, the long irons and driver should be avoided since they require a very good contact to produce any good shots. The whole essence of practice is to create new confidence, not to dissipate it.

One final word! Do not go on for too long when the exercise may well become boring. The mind loses its clarity of purpose and the muscles get tired eventually.

Practise your short game

Before outlining ways of practising the short game it is important to first point out that the ball will respond to the clubface as with all shots and that the clubface can be varied tremendously at impact. It can be in its normal position, square with the makers' loft, closed or open, strong, with the loft decreased, or weak when the loft has been increased. The great players vary the clubface position at impact through all the above dimensions to suit the shot required.

Under normal circumstances when you have short shots to play, you should first look at the ball to see what sort of lie you have, and then at the flag. You would then visualize how you want the ball to behave and select the club that would most easily give you the desired flight and roll. In many situations the execution of the shot would be kept as simple as possible, swinging the clubhead through the ball with the hands and arms letting the clubface do the job for which you have selected it.

What you require are means of developing feel since method without feel will avoid mishits but will rarely get the ball close to the hole – the main object of the exercise. The variants we have at our disposal, which determine how the ball will perform, are the clubface, the speed of the swing and the length of the swing.

To point out the two extremes, if you are playing a shot that is less than a full shot you can increase the loft of the club at address and make a full swing at much less than your normal speed. You will end up with a shot of less distance than the club would normally hit the ball but with the ball flying on a higher trajectory which flies slowly and lands very quietly. The other alternative would be to address the ball with the clubface loft somewhat decreased and using a

If you have difficulty in the short game with making good contact between club and ball follow this simple exercise. By placing a second ball a predetermined distance behind the one you intend to hit the desired angle of attack will be achieved. This second ball assists the address position by moving your weight more to the left side with your hands slightly ahead of the ball

To play a high soft shot, play the ball forward in the stance and, keeping the hands level with the ball, increase the loft on the clubface. Then use a full but slower swing than normal, and the ball will fly high and land softly

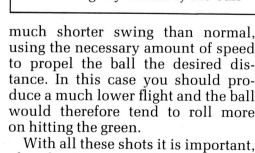

For a lower running shot, play the ball nearer the right foot than normal and keep your hands ahead of the ball, decreasing the loft on the clubface. From a shorter swing than normal you will produce the desired shot

much shorter swing than normal, using the necessary amount of speed to propel the ball the desired distance. In this case you should produce a much lower flight and the ball would therefore tend to roll more on hitting the green.

With all these shots it is important, after having selected the club, to sense the length and speed of swing, and also the amounts of wrist, arm

Most golfers have no problems with playing chip and run shots, but when height is required there is a lack of confidence. A good practice aid for lofted pitch shots is to play to an upturned receptacle such as a bucket. Just increase the club loft and play the ball slightly more forwards with the hands opposite the clubhead. Do not concentrate too much on the method. Instead, try to visualize the flight of the ball

and body action that will produce the necessary shot. Pitching and chipping are a little more difficult than the standard shots since you have this added problem of how long to swing and how hard to hit. It is the development of these aspects that the short game requires and therefore practice becomes doubly important.

If you are someone who finds difficulty in actually making good contact with the club and ball, one of the best exercises is to position a second ball behind the one you are intending to strike. For the simple chip this should be twelve to fourteen inches behind since the angle of approach of the club is relatively shallow, but for the higher pitch shot this second ball should be positioned some seven to nine inches behind the ball. In each case the very presence of the second ball will assist the address position and move the weight on to the left side with the hands slightly ahead of the ball so that in the backswing the club will climb the necessary amount to give the desired angle of attack. This feeling should obviate the most common fault of scooping the shot whereby the bottom of the arc is arrived at behind the ball, resulting in either a fluffed or topped shot.

Spend time pitching shots into a receptacle. This can be anything from a bucket to an upturned umbrella, but it does have the considerable advantage of painting a picture of how the ball should fly. Most golfers can play the chip and run fairly easily, but immediately height is required there is a certain lack of confidence resulting in a quick *independent* flick of the club which can be disastrous.

Whenever you need more height on a shot the loft angle needs to be increased and therefore the ball will be played slightly more forward with the hands opposite the clubhead. For extreme height the clubface would also be open and the swing path out-to-in. To compete with a friend or friends is quite the best practice since to some extent it takes the mind off the method and aims it more at visualizing the flight of the ball which is so desirable.

Another good exercise, again to be indulged in in a competitive way, would be to pick a spot a certain distance from the flag (between forty and 120 yards) and play shots from the same distance with various clubs. This helps enormously to gain an appreciation of how the clubface can be varied along with the speed and length of the swing to give the desired result. Past generations were rather better at what is suggested than the modern player who automatically takes a wedge for all these shots and never quite develops the right feel. Severiano Ballesteros comes to mind immediately as someone who learnt his fantastic short game by practice and making one club hit all sorts of different shots.

Lots of fun, and also of great benefit, is to compete from different places and distances with the same club, as opposed to the same distance with varying clubs. The lies and degrees of difficulty should all vary, again to develop feel. When playing, obviously you use the club that will do the job most easily, but if feel has been developed by the above suggestion the results will be much improved.

Soft shots

Along with modern architecture, and this applies particularly in the United States, most greens are elevated to some extent, to help with the drainage and overall construction of the greens. This means that many of the short shots are played to an elevated green and thus the ball pitches on the green flying at a much lower effective trajectory than if the green was at the same height as the player. It becomes doubly important therefore to be able to hit 'soft' shots, whereby at impact the loft of the club has been increased. Most players tend to de-loft the lofted clubs too much at address for these high shots, and either mishit the shot by trying to put on extra height in the hitting area or they will settle for going beyond the flag. Pitching balls to an elevated target should also become part of the exercise and also playing shots to a green set below.

In this latter situation the ball will strike the green at an increased trajectory and will usually finish some distance short of the hole.

All of the above is most beneficial and if practice can be done with like-minded friends, not only is it most helpful but it is also tremendous fun.

Chapter 7 THE MIND GAME

During a three-hour round of golf, you will spend only two or three minutes actually striking the ball. The remaining time, therefore, leaves your mind open to all kinds of distractions, mental pressures and negative thoughts. Training your mind to work for you rather than against you on the golf course is a major factor in improving *your game. Concentration is not something that can be produced at will, but this chapter can help you to guide your thought processes in the right direction, show you how to control your emotions and your scores, how to learn from your mistakes, how to conquer any first-tee nerves, and deal with both triumphs and disasters.*

Setting goals that are right for you

Going to play golf with a colleague, you might arrive at the course with a minute to spare before your teeing off time. As you dash to the tee, a par-3, you turn to your partner and say: "I will be happy as long as I get the ball off the tee and keep out of bad trouble."

You have had no time for a warm-up, so your expectations are low. You duly tee off and land the ball just 10 yards short of the pin.

Your partner is quick to respond: "Well done, you've hit it straight at the flag."

Your reply is: "Yes, but if only I'd taken one more club I'd be right on the flag."

"Changed your mind already, eh?" he replies.

He is quite right. At the outset, you set yourself a target of staying out of trouble, which you certainly achieved. Then, instead of being pleased about your success you bemoaned the fact that you had not hit a perfect shot. But you had not set out to hit one – somewhere between striking the ball and seeing where it landed, you changed your mind and decided you wanted to hit the ball as well as, if not better than, a pro.

You changed your goal. Instead of being pleased that you had exceeded the initial goal you set for yourself, you were feeling dissatisfied because you had not achieved perfection.

Setting goals is a vital and much neglected component of improving your golf. If you pay no attention to your goals, so that they are not clearly visualized and defined, the result is low motivation and slow learning. If you set them haphazardly, then the effects can include loss of confidence, failure, fear of failure and frustration and boredom. If you have ever felt as if you cannot be bothered on the golf course, you are losing confidence or are afraid of what might happen, then

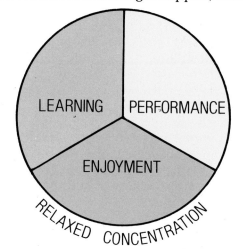

So much rests on enjoying your golf. When you enjoy what you are doing you learn through relaxed concentration. However, when over-concerned with performance, relaxed concentration disappears and your performance, enjoyment and learning ability suffer

the chances are that some attention on the goals you set yourself would be helpful.

We can divide the pitfalls in setting goals into three types: setting them too high, too low, and not defining them clearly enough.

Let us look at lack of definition first. Often when a golfer is asked what he or she would like from a lesson, the reply will be: "I want to improve" – a very worthwhile goal.

Picture Albert who is hooking the ball. He and his coach work together for a while and he hits the ball straighter.

The coach asks: "Is that OK?"

"Yes, but it's not far enough," Albert replies.

So they continue for a while longer until he hits it 10 yards further and again the coach asks: "Is that what you wanted?"

"Yes," says Albert, "but I'm still not swinging smoothly."

Every time Albert achieved a sub-goal, e.g. hitting the ball straighter, he would immediately shift the main goal further ahead and then say, "Yes, but look at what I haven't achieved."

It is easy for Albert to ignore his success and shift his goal forward because originally it was so ill-defined. "I want to improve" actually meant, "I want to hit it straighter, further and more smoothly." He was trying to achieve three things at once – a sure recipe for failure.

Setting goals too high often masquerades under the guise of "I must be perfect." You set goals for yourself which, if you take time to think about them, are just not realistic. You attempt to hit the ball just that little bit further, and a bit further, until before you know it you are trying to hit the ball as far as Ballesteros. You even expect to do it as often as he does.

Setting a goal that high or that far ahead means that you are tending to experience failure. The more often you experience failure, the less confident and more frustrated you become. When you ask yourself to do something you do not think you can achieve, you respond by trying harder – usually too hard. Trying too hard produces over-tightening, which produces error, which produces trying harder.

Copying the pros

When we ask ourselves (or are instructed) to hit the ball in a way we doubt we can really do, we try too hard. Copying the way pros hit the ball can sometimes cause this. Although the pro may take a full backswing, your body does not have the years of practice and stretching that his has, so you cannot immediately get the club back to where you want it. Because of this you then think that you will not be able to hit the ball well and so try harder. Once again you are back in that vicious circle of trying too hard, making errors and trying harder.

If setting goals too high can cause loss of confidence and failure, what happens when you set them too low? Then they are so easy to achieve that the challenge and stimulation go out of the game.

Getting the ball up in the air is an immense challenge to some beginners. They will be delighted every time it gets off the ground. However, this would be very boring for someone who has played for any length of time. Goals that are too low create boredom and low motivation. So,

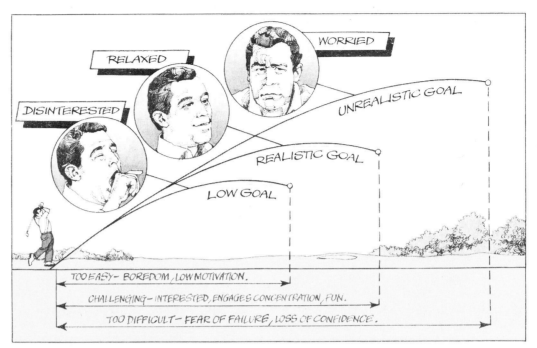

what should you do when setting goals?

1 Be specific: make sure that the goal is defined in a way that can be measured as accurately as possible. If your goal is to be consistent, define how consistent. How small an area must you land the ball in? How many times in a row and with what type of swing?

2 One goal at a time: being specific will help you sort out whether or not you are attempting too much, or have incompatible goals.

A group of golfers once tried to hit one ball with a 3-iron into a track 20 feet wide in front of them. All, except one, hit the ball over 150 yards and missed the track. The winner was the man who hit the ball with a very gentle swing 20 yards right down the middle of the track. On hearing the complaints from the others, he politely pointed out that they had introduced other goals into the exercise. They had assumed that the coach meant them to hit the track with a full shot, which made it more difficult to be accurate. Remember that there is no point setting a goal you do not think you can achieve. Get some success under your belt and then re-set your goal.

Setting yourself a realistic goal for a round of golf will add to the challenge yet take nothing away from the fun. Unrealistic goals can result in boredom or loss of confidence

3 Check to make sure they are realistic.

4 Set and forget: once you have set the goal forget about it until afterwards. There is no point in worrying about the outcome of what you are about to do. That will only disturb your concentration and create tension.

5 Review: after each round or each week, whichever is appropriate, see whether you are getting closer to your goals. Do you need to set them higher or lower next time?

6 Write them down: it is so obvious that it usually gets overlooked. Writing them down commits you to them and, then, being specific stops you from changing your mind.

7 Finally, goals should be used to put challenge, interest and direction into your game. They should never be allowed to rule you. So occasionally it might be worth asking yourself – what do I want when I next play?

Conquer those first-tee nerves

It is doubtful whether there is a golfer playing who has not experienced first-tee nerves at some time or other. Beginners often experience them when they first get on the course. High handicappers are likely to encounter them in their first few monthly medals. Low handicappers might suffer when they first attract a crowd around the first tee, and everyone is prone to an attack when they go into the last round of a tournament leading the field.

First-tee nerves sometimes start before you actually get on the first tee and can last for several holes. The most common signs to watch for are butterflies in the stomach, talking more or less than usual, shallow breathing and tense muscles. It is, of course, the tense muscles that do all the damage, because they affect your level of control over your swing.

So what causes first-tee nerves and how can you control them? First of all, you should recognize that nervousness can be helpful at times, and in the right amount. Nerves pump adrenaline into your system, making you alert and ready for action. It is only when you become too nervous that you experience the destructive effects.

The most common underlying cause of first-tee nerves is fear in some shape or form: fear or failing in some way; or fear of looking foolish. It often starts as a niggling little doubt at the back of the mind that, under pressure, becomes amplified until it is all you can think about.

Here are some typical examples of those niggling little doubts:

"I haven't played in a long time, I'm

not sure that I can hit this ball straight."

"I hope I don't miss this shot," which, in time, becomes: "Don't hit this one to the right," and usually ends up as: "Now see what you've done!"

Another common one is: "They all look so much better than me and everyone is watching. I'd better hit this well." This becomes: "Don't miss it or you'll look stupid," which turns into: "Be careful," and finally: "Why did you duff it?"

All too often what fear does is actually to cause the very thing you were afraid of originally. When you are worried about making a mistake with your first shot, you over-tighten

your muscles in your effort not to make that error and you think too much – your mind becoming too busy to concentrate fully. The result is that you invariably hit a poor shot, which is what you were afraid of doing in the first place.

Fear of looking foolish is admitted to much less often than probably occurs. After all, nobody wants to appear foolish! Not that it happens very often. Your fellow players' reaction to you having a bad day is usually a sympathetic one. They have all been through it themselves more than once. However, when you are in the thick of it, you forget that and become embarrassed about how you appear to others and fearful of making any more

mistakes. So what can you do about first-tee nerves when, and if, they strike?

Dealing with first-tee nerves

Firstly, you should recognize that fear is concern about what might happen – that is, the future. (It has not happened yet and it does not have to happen.) It may justify itself by recalling past mistakes and then saying "watch you don't do that again". Your attention is then locked into the worst thing that might happen. However, to hit the ball consistently well you need to have your attention firmly in the here and now, so that you can see and feel what you are doing.

To do this, you can draw on your past experience to help you. Most of us have been through situations where we became nervous or fearful in the past – going to the dentist, making a speech, job interviews, etc. When you became anxious at those times you would usually take several deep breaths, and, of course, some people do this on the tee. But you can extend it to your swing as well. When you are nervous you may often hold your breath as you swing down through the ball (some people do this all the time anyway) and this can cause those destructive over-tense muscles. If you make sure that you breathe out as you move through the downswing, then you have to relax the muscles in order to breathe. If

your breath comes out in a jerky fashion then you need to ensure that on the next shot you breathe out with a smooth 'whooooosh'. So, one effect of breathing out is that your muscles relax. Another is that in order to concentrate on exhaling you have to stop thinking about the future – fearing making a mistake. You cannot think about two things at once, i.e. the mistakes in the *future* and your breath *now*.

Another approach to overcoming these nerves is to trick the mind for five seconds – it is really a form of role playing. If you are afraid of hooking the ball into the rough, for example, you can use your imagination to help yourself. After all, it is your imagination that is causing the nerves – you imagine you might make a mistake. What you do is to imagine that you have already hit the ball into the rough. In other words, you have already made your mistake. There is no more need to worry because it has already happened. So now you can go ahead and hit the ball freely because what you were afraid of has already happened.

Finally, a couple of more general points. Firstly, if you notice that you are getting nervous long before you are on the tee, you should do something to occupy yourself – read a book, talk to somebody, watch TV, anything that takes your mind off the future. Secondly, do not demand perfection on that first tee shot. If you lower your goals and, for example, instead of taking a driver and aiming to cut off the tricky dog-leg, use only an iron and take the longer way round, then there is less to be afraid of!

Control your emotions and your scores

'**I**f you can meet with triumph and disaster, and treat these two imposters just the same ...' If you have ever followed the tennis at Wimbledon you may be familiar with those words. It is a quote from Rudyard Kipling's poem, 'If', and it is inscribed over the entrance to the centre court at Wimbledon. It has given many a competitor food for thought. You will notice that Kipling was referring to human endeavour rather than tennis, and what he wrote also applies to you on the golf course.

Many golfers, professionals and amateurs alike, for one reason or another, find great difficulty meeting disaster, or for that matter triumph, with any degree of composure. Like most aspects of the inner game, you have probably experienced similar situations yourself at some time. You notice that you are playing well. You work out that if you continue to play this way you will probably win the tournament or medal, and even accept the prize. Of course, your concentration has now changed from the way it was when you started playing and you are less likely to play well. Or you might get concerned about what will happen if you cannot maintain the same form. The prospect of triumph is just too much.

Maintaining composure in the face of disaster can be even more difficult and certainly is more common. Our reactions to disaster can include anger, frustration, and disappointment. We tighten our muscles in order to keep control of ourselves, but all that does is lock us up. It is as if we are semi-paralysed, unable to produce the movement we want. When we

dwell on and off through the day on how awful disaster can be, we can become almost semi-conscious. We hit the ball but do not remember doing it, we do not have any enthusiasm and the prospect of playing today just makes us want to stay in bed.

How you deal with triumph and disaster is often the measure of how much of your inherent abilities you will eventually use. Acceptance of those ups and downs is one of the key factors in performing at your best. Beware of thinking that this means being complacent because nothing could be further from the truth. Let us get a little more specific.

If you are unwilling to accept a score of, say, 90 you are likely to find it much more difficult to break 80. Your concern about your score approaching 90 makes you over-tighten your muscles as you try harder. Over-tightening of muscles, as we well know, will cause an error which takes you closer to 90 and consequently makes them tighten even more. The more unwilling you are to accept a high score the more difficult it becomes to have the loose muscles required to shoot a low score.

You need to be willing to accept that you will shoot a high score sometimes. Accepting those high scores

JERRY TEES OFF AT THE 3RD

IF I PLAY ANY MORE HOLES AS BADLY AS THE FIRST, I'LL NEVER STAY UNDER 90, LET ALONE BEAT 80. USELESS!

OH NO! IT'S IN THE WATER, IDIOT!

changes the way your body responds, allowing your muscles to stay looser and making the possibility of shooting 70 much higher. Your unwillingness to accept a score of 90 is likely to limit you to not getting below 80. Conversely, being willing to shoot 100 can give a freedom that allows you to break 80.

In attempting to be more accepting of triumph and disaster, it is often useful to take a look at the choices available to you in these situations. What seems to be the easiest option is to get angry and frustrated. In a sense, you allow negative thoughts to take over. Imagine that another golfer is your negative thoughts and he is standing next to you all the time you are playing golf. All he ever says to you are things like: "How can you play like that?"; "Now it'll be more difficult, because you've just dropped another shot"; "That's really awful, you know you can do better"; "Don't miss this one."

You have two choices. You can get into an argument with him about how he should be quiet and leave you alone. How he should not say things like that. How it is not fair. You can tense your muscles, shout and generally waste enormous amounts of energy on him.

The alternative is to ignore him and make the best of a bad job. You accept that the situation is not ideal but *it is* the situation. He is shouting at you, making it very difficult for you to relax and concentrate and you just have to accept it and get used to it. It is similar to accepting the noise of traffic if you live near a road. If you live in the countryside that level of noise is unacceptable but in the city it is all right. You have to make up your mind that nothing he does or says will make any difference to you. You take on the attitude that *you* choose. You accept that he is there, you give yourself your best chance by ignoring him, and you hit the ball. *T*hen you accept the result because you know you gave it your best 'shot'.

This is a simple model for all those negative thoughts. What you have to accept is that what has happened has happened, whether you like it or not. If you accept that it has happened, you can move forward on to the next shot. If you do not accept it, you trap yourself in the past. Your mind often diverts you from accepting the situation by reading too much into it. One dropped stroke is interpreted as "I can't achieve the score I wanted". But if you look at the successful pros' cards what do you find? They drop shots quite often. However, they *accept* them as part of a round.

Obviously it takes practice – conscious practice – but it can be well worth the effort. Acceptance is often what allows you to meet with triumph and disaster and treat those two imposters just the same!

Acceptance of your own human fallibility is the way to overcome mistakes early in your round and help you on your way to lower scores. Being overly critical of yourself only creates tension and leads to even more bad shots

'Feel' your way to better shots

"I know what I'm doing wrong, I just can't seem to correct it."

"I know what I have to do, now I must put in the hours on the practice ground to get it right."

"I've been to several pros and read lots of books and they all tell me to do the same thing and I still cannot get myself to do it."

Sometimes when you are developing your game you know exactly what you want to do but just cannot seem to get it to happen consistently. Typically, our old friend Steven Slicer might watch his ball curve out to the right of where he is aiming and say to himself, "Ah ha, the ball started out to the left of the target and curved even more to the right. My clubface must have been open to the target at impact and my swing path must have been out-to-in. To correct that I'll try to make sure I don't do that again. I'll also work harder on my swing path in practice."

On the practice ground Steven is to be found busily hitting the balls, analysing what must have happened after each shot and trying to do the right things. Sometimes he manages to hit the ball the way he wants to, but more often it is a process of becoming more and more frustrated.

What is happening to Steven is that he is using analysis as a substitute for feel. He is so busy analysing what he must have done wrong on each shot that he is not doing anything to increase his feel of what he is actually doing. In fact, in some respects his analysis is reducing his awareness of what he is actually doing.

Perhaps the best way to explain this is with an example. Some time ago, European Tour pro David Feherty asked for help with his swing. He had been working very hard on changing his grip the previous season, and recently had been working on improving his swing, but he found that he was not hitting the ball nearly as accurately as he wanted to. After each shot he could work out what must have gone wrong, but it seemed pointless trying to correct that because on the next shot it would be something else that was wrong. Obviously he knew what he should do in order to

Over-analysis is rarely productive and can lead to a lack of feel

hit the ball well, but probably he was unable to *feel* what he should do because he was unable to *sense* the movement of his club and body to the degree that he normally did.

Asking him to alter anything in his swing would have been pointless. He already knew what he needed to do but could not get it to happen. He needed to feel more accurately what he was doing. His coach asked him to hit some balls and sure enough they went all over the place. The coach then asked him what was the noticeable thing about what he did when he swung. He hit some more balls and replied: "It doesn't feel quite right."

"OK, that's how it doesn't feel, now hit some more and tell me how it *does* feel!"

"Uncomfortable," he said.

"Where in your body do you feel uncomfortable – which bit of you is uncomfortable?"

He hit some more balls and replied, "hands and arms."

"Be more specific. What is it about your hands and arms?" He hit some more balls and said, "I seem to be using an awful lot of effort," and after a few more he added, "and they are moving fast."

Most effective tempo

At this stage he was getting interested in the feel of his hands and arms and visibly relaxing. The next few balls contained much less effort, which allowed his swing to slow down to his most effective tempo and enabled him to hit the ball much more accurately. By asking him questions about what he was actually doing, his attention was drawn away from the analysis of the last shot, and his 'should' about how to correct it. Not only that but his attention was now on what *really* mattered, i.e. what he was *actually* doing. Once he concentrated on this, he began to 'feel' more of how his body was moving and was then *able* to correct it.

Feeling the movement of your body requires you to pay attention to the sensation of the movements. Thinking about what you have analysed

To stimulate feel, concentrate on what you are doing rather than what you think you are doing

from the last shot fills up your attention so much that there is no room left to feel what is happening now. However, the analysis does have an important function – it tells you the area in which to increase your feel, so that you use the analysis to *direct* your attention. Let us rejoin Steven Slicer for a while.

He is still slicing balls out to the right and has analysed that he is not releasing his hands through the ball, i.e. his clubhead is behind his hands at impact. Ask him to focus his attention on his hands and say whether there is any release at all. Ask him also to forget about trying to stop the slice, to let the ball go anywhere and just find out whether there is any release. He hits eight balls and says,

"Yes, there was some on three of them." Actually he is only giving less attention to analysing and more to feeling what is actually happening. "Now tell me after every ball how much release there was on a scale of 0–5, 0 being none and 5 a lot," you say. He reports back, "One, zero, zero, three, one, two, three, five, four, three, four, five, four. Oh, it's relaxing." As he kept his attention he began to feel more and conversely, the more he kept analysing what he should do, the less he felt.

So, analysis has its place as it tells you what went wrong. However, in itself it does not increase feel. To increase feel, you have to *sense* your movement by paying attention to how the movement feels *as* you do it.

How your game can gain from competition

That competition creates some interesting situations for people is probably a huge understatement. So for those of you that get anxious and over-concerned about winning, here is the secret of how to win every time. If your main purpose in playing competitively is to win and you find it unacceptable to lose, then follow this advice. Always play in a field much worse than you!

If you are disappointed in this secret then it could be that winning is not everything for you. Probably playing well is much more important to you, so much so that you would quite likely rather play well and lose than play badly and win. You want the winning to be an indication of your own level of performance, not your opponent's lack of it.

Yet how many of us have found ourselves hoping that our partners or opponents miss putts?

What we are doing is asking our fellow-players to be bad players for a while so that we can win. This means that your winning does not indicate that you have played well – only that they played badly. You want to play against good players so that winning means something, and then you hope that they will play like bad players. Your thinking can get confused under the pressure of competitive play.

However, sometimes this process is more gradual. When you first take up the game of golf, almost without exception it is for enjoyment. The enjoyment comes in many forms: for example, exercise, meeting people, learning a new skill, getting away from work, husband or wife, doing business or even (especially with youngsters) the sheer joy of hitting balls.

When you do things in this state of mind, you tend to be relaxed, very easy going and undemanding of yourself. In this state of mind, a great deal of learning takes place, largely at a subconscious level, your level of performance increases rapidly and you improve quickly.

At some stage you will notice that you have improved a lot and decide that you must not slip back, especially now that you are entering competitions. You might have one bad round and start to worry about whether you have lost your touch. You are beginning to concentrate more on your performance (or call it your results if you like) and much less on the enjoyment of your golf. The consequence of this is that your learning rate slows down and so does your rate of improvement, making you put even more emphasis on performance, and so on.

This effect happens most frequently in beginners after a few months, and professionals after they have just turned professional or have been competing for many years. Many pros say that on turning professional they decided they had to be serious about their game because it had become their living. They confuse seriousness with dedication and professionalism, neither of which excludes enjoyment.

JACK, TOM & RAYMOND ON THE WAY TO THE SECOND TEE......

I HATE TO LOSE, SO I'M OK WITH JACK & TOM. I CAN PLAY BADLY AND STILL BEAT THEM BOTH

RAY'S GOOD, BUT I'M LEARNING FROM HIM, AND THE WAY I'M IMPROVING I'LL BE TAKING ON THE SINGLE HANDICAPPERS NEXT YEAR

IF I PLAY MY BEST I CAN BEAT JACK BUT NOT RAY. STILL, I REALLY ENJOY THE COMPETITION AND FOR A RELATIVE BEGINNER I'M DOING WELL

Different people play golf for different reasons – make sure you play for the right ones!

In this exercise the left arm, although losing the battle, gains more than the right because it has to expend 100 per cent of its strength. Thus, you should always try to compete against superior players if you want to improve quickly

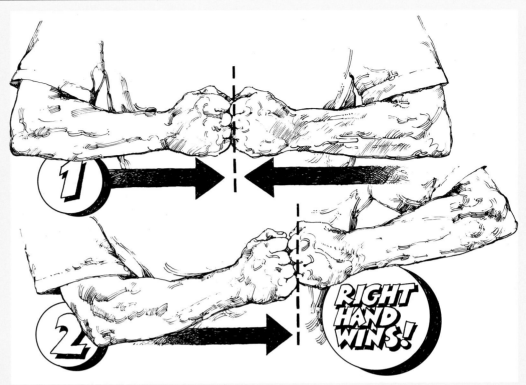

Wanting something you may not get produces anxiety, and consequently high performance is something you may not achieve. So over-emphasis on performance can produce this effect – the golfer's nightmare.

Very often redressing the balance between learning, performance and enjoyment can produce significant results. An example that often occurs is the volume of practice. Some professionals put in so many hours of drudgery on the practice ground in the belief that they will play better for it that their enthusiasm gradually disappears. When they cut down their volume of practice, they enjoy playing more, they learn more, and more rapidly, and their performance improves.

A closer look at what is to be gained from playing competitively can often be useful. Try pushing your two hands together (see the illustration). The winner of this little competition is whichever hand can push the other one back outside the line of your body. If, say, your right hand wins, especially if you are right-handed, your reaction to your right hand is to treat it well, wash it, take care of it and think it is terrific. Your reaction to your left hand is to ignore it or even criticize it for its poor performance.

What else is happening here besides the immediately visible win and loss? What do you actually gain from doing the exercise? One thing is that your arms are going to grow stronger, but which arm is going to gain more strength?

The answer is your left arm. Think about it. Because your right arm is much stronger than your left arm it only had to use a proportion of its effort in order to win – let us say it had to put out 60 per cent of its full effort. But your left arm had to put out 100 per cent of its effort in a bid to win, and physically you gain more strength the more effort you exert.

So although your left arm lost the competition, it actually gained more strength or more improvement than your right arm. It may have lost the battle but it is in better shape for the war. Psychologically, the effect is the same. The tougher the competition you are up against, the more difficult the circumstances, then the more you can actually learn and improve *if* you put in your full effort, i.e. you do not quit, make excuses, lose your temper or indulge in any of the other many ways of avoiding what you do not like.

Yes, of course nobody likes to lose or play badly, but the stress and anxiety can be reduced by remembering how much there is to be gained for the future out of the difficulties you are encountering right now. What it requires is persistence in giving 100 per cent effort.

Below is a brief list of some of the benefits you can gain from competing.

During play
Exercise
Enjoyment
Improvement
Developing concentration
Developing self-confidence
Developing control under pressure

After winning
Trophy or money
Status
Pride of achievement
Better self-image
Approval of others

You will notice that the most lasting benefits come from what you do during the game. Those gained after winning tend to be more transient.

So if you are going to play competitively, and you find it gets you down, remember:

1 Be clear why you are playing. It was supposed to be for fun!
2 Do not get sidetracked. Do not change your mind midway.
3 Competing strengthens many facets of your game if you persist with your maximum effort.

INDEX

Numerals in *italics* refer to illustrations

A
Address, relaxing at, 12-13, *76*
  in downhill bunker shots, 83
Advancing years, combating, 142-43
Aiming, 18-19
Alignment, 18-19

B
Backswing, 22, 38, *39*, 40-41
  action of feet and legs in, *43*
  and avoiding overswing, 120
  and correcting toeing, 105
  and curing the shank, 124
  in downhill shots, 85
  faults in, 44
  and pulling, 119, *119*
  in the rough, 134, 135
  and separation between hands, *108*
  and smothering, 111
Bad lies, 16, *60*, 61, 64
Ball flight, laws of, 56-57
Ball position, 16, 58
Ballesteros, Severiano, *12, 63, 134,*
  147
  putting sequence, *89*
  swing sequence, *34*
Barnes, Brian, 24
Brand, Gordon, Jnr,
  swing sequence, *37*
Bunker(s), 74-85
  downhill shots from, 82-85
  edge of, 133, *133*
  judging length, 78-81
  long shots from, 81, *80*
  plugged in, 133, 138-39

C
Casting, *108*
Charles, Bob,
  swing sequence, *28-29*
Chipping, 62-65, 66-69
Closed stance, *57*
Clover, playing from, 135
Club selection, 55, 63-64, 66-67, 143
Coles, Neil, 149
Combined downhill and side slopes,
  130
Crenshaw, Ben, *13*, 24

  and backswing, *121*
Cross slopes, 130

D
Direction of long pitch, 71-72
Distance, knowing your, 54-55
Divot mark, ball in, 137
Downhill lies, 129-30, *131*
Downhill putts, 137-38
Downhill shots, 82-85, 129-30
Drivers, 17, 52
Driving, 50-53

E
Equipment, 16-17
Exercises, for muscles, 20-21, *20-21*

F
Fairway shots, *16*
Fairway woods, 17, 58-61
Faldo, Nick, *13, 24, 150*
  swing sequence, *28-29*
Fern, playing from, 135
Foot action, 42-45, *42-43*
Forearms, strengthening, 20, *21*
Forward press, 91
Frozen action pictures, 114

G
Gaps, firing through, 139
Goals, 148-49
Good lies, 17, 64
Graham, David, *61*
Gravel path, playing from, 133
Grip, 10, 14-15
  checking, *14*, 14-15
  in hooking, *96*, 96-97, 141
  left-hand, 14
  putting, 86, *86-87*
  reverse overlap, *87*
  right-hand, 15
  and the slice, 94
  Vardon, *15*

H
Hands, strengthening, *20*
Heather, playing from, 135
Hit impulse, 22-23

Hitting behind the ball, 108-109
Hogan, Ben, 149
Hooking, 96-97, 108, 129, 130, *131,*
  correct way to, *140*, 140-41
  curing a, 96
Hunt, Bernard, *19, 61*

I
Impact, simple approach to, 46
Irons, 16-17

J
Jacklin, Tony, 149
Jogging, 20
Jones, Ernest, 48

L
Langer, Bernhard, *67, 70, 84*
  swing sequence, *26-27*
Late hit, myth of, 114-15
Legs, action of, 42-44, *42-43*
Legs, strengthening, 20, *21*
Length, judging, 78-81
Lies, 17, 64
  bad, 16, *60*, 61, 64
  bare, 69, *132*, 132-33
  downhill, 129-30, *131*
  good, 17, 64
  poor, 132-35
  tight, *133*
  uneven, *128-31*
  uphill, 129, *129*
Lining up, 18-19, 53
Links courses, 128-29
Long irons, 16-17
Long pitch shots, 70-73
Lyle, Sandy,
  swing sequence, *35*

M
Marsh, Graham, *134*
Middle irons, 16
Miller, Johnny, *61*
Muscles, 12, 152

N
Nerves, conquering, 150-51
Nicklaus, Jack, 10, 15, *38, 78, 90,* 114,

120, *135*
    swing sequence, *32*
Norman, Greg, *50*, 51
    swing sequence, *23*

O
Open stance, *56*, 128
Overswing, avoiding an, 120-23

P
Pace and rhythm, 41
Pacing the course, 54
Palmer, Arnold, *79*
Pate, Jerry, *105*
Pitch shots, 70-71, *147*
    long, 70-73
    low-flying, 72-73
    standard, 70-71
Player, Gary, 13, *74*, *90*, *108*, *110*
    swing sequence, *24-25*
Plugged shots, 77
Plumb-bobbing, *92*
Positioning the ball, 16-17
    in hooking, 97
    and set-up, 58
Posture, 10, 13
    during address, 13
Practice, the point of, 46-47, 144-47
    for curing the shank, 125
Practice putts, *91*
Practice tips, 19
Practising the short game, 146-47
Pre-shot movements, 13
Pre-shot routines, 12-13
Pulling, corrections for, 119
    eradicating, 116-17
Pushing, 100-101
Putting, 86-93
    downhill, 137-38

R
Relaxation at address, 12-13
Rough, playing from, 133-35
    deep-, 135
    medium-, 134-35
    semi-, 134
    wet, 134
Royal St George's, 128

S
St Andrews, 128
Sand, hard, 77
Sand wedge, 66, 74
Scooping, 104, *105*
Scoring, 50
Selection of clubs, 55, 63-64, 66-67
Setting-up, 10-11, 144
    and aim, 10-11
    and bunker shots, 74
    and chipping, 62
    and posture, 10
    relaxation during, 12-13
Shank, curing the, 124-25
Short irons, 16
Shut stance, 128
Side-spin, 57
Skied shots, *17*, *98*, *99*
Skipping, 20
Skying, avoiding, 98-99
Slicing, *94-95*, 99, 129, 130, 144, *145*
    correct way to, 140-41
Smothered shots, *17*, 110-13
Snead, Sam, 10, 24
Soft shots, *147*
Spin, 57
Stance,
    closed, *57*
    open, *56*, 128
    shut, 128
Standing,
    above the ball, 130
    below the ball, 130
Strange, Curtis,
    swing sequence, *45*
Swaying, how to stop, 100, *101*
Swing, the, 22-25, 26, 36, *48*
    adjusting with age, 142-43
    for bunker shots, 74
    for a driver, 52
    essence of a good, 38-41
    key to a good, 10-11
    with woods, 58-59

T
Target, lining up a, 18, 19
Tempo, 22-25, *145*, 155
Thomson, Peter, 46

Toeing, 102-105
Torrance, Sam, 24, *144*
Trevino, Lee, 12, 61, 137
    swing sequence, *30-31*
Trouble, getting out of, 136-39

U
Uneven lies, 128-31
Up and over chip, 66-69
Uphill lies, 129
Uphill shots, 129

V
Vardon grip, *15*

W
Wadkins, Larry, 24
Waites, Brian, 24
Watson, Tom, 24, *43*, *63*, *87*, *135*
    swing sequence, *33*
Weight distribution, 42-43
Weight transference, 44
Wind direction, 55
Wrist cock delay, 122
Wrists, strengthening, *20*

Z
Zoeller, Fuzzy, *75*

Acknowledgements

Photographs
We would like to thank the following for supplying photographic material for use in the book:

Ken Adwick: pages 104, 105, 113, 136, 137, 138 and 139
Richard Darcey: page 9
Peter Dazeley: pages 12, 19, 23, 24-25, 30-31, 32, 33, 45, 46, 47, 61 and 76
Keith Hailey: page 47
Ken Lewis: pages 37, 52 and 53
Lawrence Levy: cover pictures (front and back) and pages 34 and 35
Phil Sheldon: pages 11, 13, 15, 28-29, 38, 43, 49, 50, 59, 63, 67, 74, 75, 77, 78, 79, 84, 87, 89, 90, 91, 92, 110, 114, 115, 118, 121, 128, 129, 131, 132, 133, 134, 135, 140, 141, 144, 150 and 155
Stephen Szurlej: pages 26-27

Illustrations
The illustrations throughout the book and on the back cover are by Ken Lewis with the exception of those in Chapter 7 which are by Dave F. Smith. They have all been supplied by the British *Golf World* Magazine.